Transition

To Contact David Werdiger, Author and Speaker:

David Werdiger
PO Box 157
Collins St West VIC 8007
AUSTRALIA

Phone Number:
+61 3 8611 1150 (GMT +10)

Email:
speaking@davidwerdiger.com

Transition

How to Prepare Your Family and Business for the Greatest Wealth Transfer in History

David Werdiger

Disclaimer: The Publisher and the Author make no representation or warranties with respect to the accuracy or completeness of the contents of this work and specifically disclaim all warranties of fitness for a particular purpose. No warranty may be created or extended by sales or promotional materials. The advice and strategies contained herein may not be suitable for every situation. This work is sold with the understanding that the Publisher is not engaged in rendering legal, accounting or other professional services. If professional assistance is required, the services of a competent professional person should be sought. Neither the Publisher nor the Author shall be liable for damages arising therefrom. The fact that an organization or website is referred to in this work as a citation and/or potential source of further information does not mean that the Author or the Publisher endorses the information the organization or website may provide or recommendations it may make. Further, readers should be aware that internet websites listed in this work may have changed or disappeared between when this work was written and when it is read.

Disclaimer: The cases and stories in this book have had details changed to preserve privacy.

This edition of Transition is written using American English terms, phrasing, and conventions.

First Edition 2017

ISBN: 978-0-9861036-7-4
ISBN: 978-0-9861036-9-8 (ebook)

Printed in the United States of America

Published by:

Lasting Press
615 NW 2nd Ave #915
Canby, OR 97013

www.DavidWerdiger.com

Cover and Interior Design by: Rory Carruthers Marketing
Project Management and Book Launch by: Rory Carruthers Marketing
www.RoryCarruthers.com

For more information about David Werdiger or to book him for your next event, speaking engagement, podcast or media interview please visit: www.DavidWerdiger.com

For my father, in my own way.

Contents

Preface

Often, people working in successful family businesses grapple with the intergenerational challenges of family and wealth. Most businesses have a mix and diversity of people. In a family business, there are often different people from different generations with different positions and different levels of power, but all from the same family. The First Generation Entrepreneur (whom I will refer to as the "1G") starts with ultimate power, but at some point, there must be a generational shift, not just in wealth, but in power. This book is for people who might be dealing with those challenges as power and authority shifts.

Transition is also for people who are dealing with power struggles on the same generational level with siblings. There's no shortage of conflict between siblings in families. As a wise man once told me, just because people happen to have been born of the same parents, doesn't mean they should get on with each other. When you throw money into the picture, that doesn't make things better, it makes it worse.

My Family's Transition

I wrote this book because I've been going through the same journey in my family. A few years ago, I realized that my family would go through this transition. I've seen other families go through it, only to struggle. I had an inkling of what was coming in my family, and I wanted to prepare for it as best I could.

I prepared for it by galvanizing my knowledge and experience of entrepreneurship, and by learning about families from a generational perspective and a philanthropic perspective; through my research, I've learned a lot. While I don't have all the answers, I'm far better prepared for what my family is now going through. I know the challenges that come with these types of transitions in our lives; I want to help others who are going through a similar challenge, preparing to go through a challenge as this transition takes place.

This book is designed to help people who are at various stages in their family journey and dealing with the possible communication challenges across multiple generations. I want to give them the knowledge and the understanding of what's going on and why it's happening, so they will be better able to deal with it. Some people might believe that the transition will happen at certain predetermined junctures in time: when this person dies, when that person turns twenty-one, or when the business is sold. People can look to various events in the future that will be triggers for these sorts of challenges, or they can already be in the middle of it.

Through this book, you will learn how to have a stronger, better connected, and more cohesive multi-generational family. You will learn how to leverage the strengths of your family unit. The family unit is one of the most ancient and enduring social constructs. It is a very powerful thing, yet at the same time, in so many cases, it's the source of conflict and divisiveness. I want people to be able to retain the positives from of their family and build generational bridges. Generation gaps are often a source of division, but on the other hand, they can be used to bring families together.

As challenging as families and family businesses can be, they can also bring great joy and meaning into our lives. Family wealth can be divisive during transitions; however, it does not need to be that way. It is possible to work together and use wealth as a source of inspiration. Wealth can lead to fulfilling pursuits and meaningful contributions in the world.

I enjoy helping others. There are many different ways to help others, and one way I do this is by sharing ideas and hoping that the ideas will switch on a lightbulb in their heads and make their lives better for it.

As you learn more about the strategies and preparations that have helped many family businesses successfully transition, please begin taking steps to apply this knowledge to your situation by completing the valuable exercises in the companion *Transition Workbook.* This workbook will allow you to have a deeper understanding of how your family business can flourish during a time of transition. Access your complimentary copy of the *Transition Workbook* at www.DavidWerdiger.com/transition-workbook

It is my sincere wish for you that the lessons I have learned by going through this generational shift with my own family bring you more connection with your family and a better understanding of how to make your family business successful for generations to come.

Introduction

I classify myself as a GenX with four Baby Boomer siblings. My parents migrated separately to Australia after World War II, and met and married in Australia. They had four children within the span of about six years. There was a gap of five years, and then I was born.

Family Dynamic

In any family, every child is born into a "different family." For example, a family might start with two people, and settle into their life together as a couple, and then a child is born, and things change. Then the family incorporates that change and shifts into a family with two parents and one child. Boom, then another child might come along. Whatever the family state, each time a child is born, the family dynamic shifts because of the addition of a new child. A similar thing happens when children grow up and leave the house; that also shifts the family dynamic.

In my case, I grew up in a very different family environment than my siblings did. My siblings are all significantly older than me—a gap of five years to eleven years. From a family wealth perspective, I don't remember a time when our family ever struggled financially. My father was already quite successful by the time I arrived; he had improved his socio-economic status significantly. We lived in a nice house, and as the youngest, and especially as the youngest after a long gap, I enjoyed many of the additional privileges associated with being the youngest. Growing up, our family never lacked for anything, which led to me having a different perspective on life than my siblings.

I think it's important to understand that even within one family, depending on the span of years between the oldest and the youngest, each member can have a very different perspective on life and on their role within the family. Because of this age gap, when I was a teenager, my siblings were already leaving home and getting married. In our family, and more broadly in the Orthodox Jewish community in which we live, children generally live at home until they marry. I felt like an only child in the family for nearly ten years between the time my sister married and when I married and moved out. All of those things meant that I felt that my position in the family was different from that of everybody else.

As a child, I was very docile. I was sheltered, naive, and just went along with everything. I went with the flow for a long time, and things just kept happening in life and in business. I didn't really stop to reflect on them or understand them until much, much later. I was a "late bloomer" and only started to think about my position in the family as I met other families and learned more about their situations, and what we had in common.

Family History

My late father survived great adversity; he survived the Holocaust. He came from a large and prominent family in Sosnowiec—a small town in Poland, near Cracow. His parents ran a successful family business and were active in their community helping others less fortunate. With the onset of the war, the eldest in the family was sent to a labor camp, and never heard from again, and a ghetto was established in Sosnowiec. The families were able to remain there for some years until the decision was finally made by the Nazis to "liquidate" it. My grandfather remained in the ghetto as part of the cleanup, and the rest of the family was sent on a train to the Auschwitz-Birkenau concentration camp. The women and younger children were "selected" for immediate death, and my father and his brother became slave laborers for IG Farben, the large German industrial conglomerate.[1]

After a time, the two sons were united with their father and remained in Auschwitz until the infamous death march in January 1945.[2] The camp was evacuated and thousands of prisoners were forced to march for weeks through the bitter cold, many dying of starvation and exposure, or shot for the crime of not marching in step. They ended up in the Buchenwald concentration camp. By this time, my father had contracted typhus and was severely ill—he was colloquially called a "muselmann"—someone waiting to die. He and his brother were liberated on April 11, 1945 by the US Army and were the sole survivors of our family. Their father was shot by the Nazis just weeks earlier.

My father convalesced for four years in a sanitorium in Switzerland—a long and difficult struggle exacerbated by the emotions of dealing with the loss of most of his family. His older brother was in far better health, and shortly after the war immigrated to New York. But even after he had completed his recovery, my

1 "IG Farben." *Wikipedia.* Wikimedia Foundation. Web.

2 "Death Marches (Holocaust)." *Wikipedia.* Wikimedia Foundation. Web.

father's health history meant he was not eligible to immigrate to the USA to be united with his brother. However, he had some cousins who had migrated to Australia from Poland before the war, and they sponsored him.

Initially in his new life in Australia in the early 1950s, his cousins took him into their business, and he was able to grow and develop the business in manufacturing and garment sales. As he enjoyed success, his cousins progressively increased his share in the business so that he would continue to stay with them, to the point where they were equal partners.

Then in the late 1960s, tragedy struck as his two cousins both died suddenly in their forties within the space of a year, leaving widows and young families. That suddenly propelled my father into a position of responsibility for both his family and their two families.

The business was in trading and fabric manufacturing. My father was something of a pioneer in this industry; he had an eye for fashion. He traveled overseas (which very few people did back then) and brought back the latest fashions. He was able to manufacture those fashions and meet a need in new local markets. It grew from there and was a very successful and large business in the 1970s and 1980s.

Something that we all want with our businesses is growth, and my father was no exception. Because of that, I grew up with my father working very long hours and regularly going on business trips. That was what I saw as a role model: not somebody who worked a nine-to-five job, rather somebody for whom business was a very important part of his life—growing a business and being a business owner. Without thinking about it too much, it seemed fairly obvious to me that I too would ultimately also have my own business.

I would occasionally work in the family business during the summer break and part-time during university studies. My brother joined the business in the 1980s, and some other family members, who were a lot older than me, also worked in the family business. I was there as the boss's son, and that felt a little odd—almost uncomfortable. I would think, "Will I one day inherit and be responsible for this business? Will the people I'm working for now one day be my employees or subordinates?" Those were the kind of thoughts that had been floating through my mind, but it was never something I discussed with anyone or considered fully.

Aside from that, I was more interested in the technology side of the business. That was what I was familiar with, rather than fashion or manufacturing. So it wasn't as if I immediately took a liking to the business and wanted to be part of it. That eventually led me to my own businesses in the technology industry.

Family Identity versus Personal Identity

I have three sisters and one brother. My family is a very classic patriarchy. After completing university studies, my brother worked elsewhere for a few years and then eventually joined the family business. The girls were never involved in the business. As the youngest, I was running "behind" the others in my life journey, and as I completed school and went to university, I was not really inclined to join the family business. I wanted to get a job using what I knew, not whom I knew. Indeed, that was something I told a girl on a date, when she asked me, "Why don't you just join the family business?" I think it impressed her.

After school, I took two years off for intensive Talmudic and Jewish theology studies: one year in Melbourne, and then in

Jerusalem. Taking at least one year off after school for this purpose was de rigeur in our community. The second year enabled me to travel and open my eyes to the world around me. Returning to Melbourne and university studies, I majored in math and computer science and took a campus leadership role—providing kosher food and organizing events for the small but close-knit group of Jewish students. I surged through the first two years, taking overload subjects (because I could) and working part-time, but in the third and final year of my degree, the momentum subsided, and I started to get itchy feet.

I was in my early twenties and living at home, which, as mentioned, was common practice in our community. As my undergraduate degree studies drew to a close, my mother wanted me to do an honors year and continue my university studies (because I could). However, I was ready to move into the workplace and start earning some money myself. In those days, a university degree with decent marks was a ticket for a job, so I applied for the first job that caught my eye, and was promptly accepted. This was exciting—I didn't want to join the family business or even rely on the family to get a job. It was a thrill to get a job on my own merits. I didn't really think about it so much at the time—it was a deep-seated instinct. I needed to prove that I could do this myself. I saw that my family had done well and that my father was a very successful businessman, but it was important to me that I could be my own person. I needed to carve my own path in the world and not just be my father's son, but be "me."

My Entrepreneurial Start

Having studied computer science, I worked initially as a software developer for a large stockbroking firm. After advancing, I took a shift within the company and spent a year in the research department as a quantitative analyst. But in the back of my mind, I was looking for opportunities because I wanted to be in business for myself. Eventually, I started importing a software development tool part-time while having a full-time job. That venture was meandering along, but I had my eye on the point when I could take that leap from employment into self-employment. Eventually, a customer who had purchased my product asked if I could also develop some custom software for them using that product. This was the moment I had been waiting for, so I dived head first into working full time on my own business.

I resigned from my analyst job and started doing custom software development for clients that I met through selling software. That was my first leap into self-employment. The business paid its way, and I had some degree of independence, but there was no plan. I went from one development job to the next. I didn't own a business; I owned a job.

It wasn't until I moved into a new office that an opportunity came out of the blue. I happened to meet somebody who was sharing the office space that I was using. This was in the mid-1990s, a time when, in Australia, the telecommunications market was being deregulated. I met a businessman who was starting a phone company. He said, "I need a billing system, and you're a software developer. Can you develop a billing system for me?" I had never developed such a system before, so I had no idea how to do it or what his specific requirements were. I replied confidently, "Absolutely."

Through this client, I met his wholesale supplier at a company called Optus, which was the newly launched second telecommunications carrier in Australia. He had said to me, "You know there are a few other companies that have got some billing challenges, perhaps you can help them?" He referred me to another emerging telco. At that point, a lightbulb went off in my head. I thought: selling my time developing software can make a living, but it's not really scalable. After all, there are only so many hours of time in the day to be sold, and even if I could be paid a large sum of money per hour, those limitations remain.

From a business perspective, you can either be selling your time or you can be selling a product, and I decided that what I actually wanted to do was be a software vendor. That way, I could develop software once and sell it many times. I saw that as a much better basis for a business, and one that has the potential for growth.

This was a time when the boom in the Australian telecommunications market was just starting. The breakthrough in the business happened when a prospective customer approached me wanting something a little different. He needed billing software, but he didn't want to pay for it. Because his was a start-up business, he didn't want to pay a huge sum up-front for a billing system. He had an alternative: to "lease" the software from me and have me operate it on his behalf. That was the birth of an important transition of the business; rather than licensing software for a large sum of money followed by trailing maintenance income stream, we would sell software on a monthly "revenue share" basis. The deal we agreed upon was that he would use the software, we would host it for him on our IT infrastructure, and we would charge him a percentage of the turnover of his business, as calculated by the billing system each month.

This was "cloud computing" and "software as a service" (SaaS) before those terms existed. This was the revenue share model for selling software, which is now ubiquitous, but in the late 1990s, it was unheard of. That shift in business model kick-started the venture because there were a lot of start-up telco companies who wanted to do just this. None of them had a lot of start-up capital to spend, and whatever money they did have would be better spent on sales and marketing, rather than on an expensive piece of software. The business model that we were using to sell billing systems fit their need as a start-up business, and that triggered some significant growth.

Family Support

All journeys have their ups and downs, and mine was no exception. During the times my business was financially challenged, my father was there as a safety net. The support—both emotional and financial—was unconditional, despite the fact that for a sustained period of time, the business would just ramble along without any real plan. That was my initial approach to business—I began with minimum planning and budgeting and ran things by the seat of my pants.

Having such a safety net in place was very significant for me. Unlike the contemporary trend of start-ups to "fail fast," having family support reinforced my self-belief and persistence to continue with my dream until I would ultimately succeed.

Family Business Transition

As a member of the family, the business that my father built greatly impacted my life. I have a lot of respect for my father's hard work and his legacy. My siblings and I all took different paths, and from time to time, we were all called upon to do our part as our family business transitioned. I learned a lot from my business experiences and studies, and realized some of that could help with the family business transition, and with the transitions I would undertake myself. I hope that the tools and wisdom presented in the following chapters will allow your multi-generational family business to thrive during its transition.

CHAPTER 1

Understanding Generational Labels

(And Why It's Important for Your Family Business)

"Each generation is reared by its predecessor; the latter must therefore improve in order to improve its successor. The movement is circular."

– Emile Durkheim

This is the first time in the history of humankind that four generations have lived concurrently. The modern era has meant people are far better off than they used to be. Life expectancies continue to increase and are much longer than even a hundred years ago. In practical terms, this means that younger generations often get to engage with their grandparents and their great-grandparents.

When we speak of generations these days, we name them. On average in the Western world, a generation is about twenty to twenty-five years. We have named each successive generation. The first generation named was the Baby Boomers. The Baby Boomers were born between the end of World War II (1945) and about 1965—a period of about twenty years. In the NPR article "From

GIs To Gen Z (Or Is It iGen?): How Generations Get Nicknames," Samantha Raphelson explores the origins of generational names. "There were the baby boomers, named to describe the economic boom after World War II and, later, the rise in fertility rates. Even the U.S. Census Bureau uses the name."[3] The end of the war signaled the start of a period with a lot more positivity in the world, and that resulted in a baby boom. After two major wars in the space of thirty years, people had confidence that the world would not end itself, and therefore, decided to have babies.

It also accompanied, though, a time of great social change in the world in the 1960s and 1970s. Baby Boomers were the first generation to be named. They're an important marker, an important generation, and social commentators have observed this cohort of Baby Boomers as they've grown up. Now we're coming to the time where some Baby Boomers are already in retirement, which has its own set of challenges, such as financial woes and increased healthcare costs. "As reality sets in, only 24% of boomers express confidence that they will have enough resources in retirement vs. 37% five years ago."[4]

Writers, journalists, and historians have coined the majority of generational names. "Coining a nickname for an entire generation has become something of a pastime for academics, journalists and marketers."[5] They've worked backward and worked forward generationally, so they've decided to call the generation that preceded the Baby Boomers the Traditionalist Generation. While Baby Boomers embraced a lot of social change, the generation that preceded them was very conservative—the ones who saw World

[3] "From GIs To Gen Z (Or Is It IGen?): How Generations Get Nicknames." *NPR.* NPR. Web.

[4] "Why Retirement Reality Is Finally Sinking In for Baby Boomers." *Time.* Time. Web.

[5] "How Generations Get Their Names." *Time.* Time. Web.

War I and World War II. They lived a far more conservative life with far less social change going on. They set the foundation for this successive generational change.

Beyond that, they've identified children of Baby Boomers as Generation X. The current youngest generation alive in the world is known as the Millennial generation, that is, the people born in the twenty-first century.

All of the generations are very broad labels because labeling is predicated on the notion that people from each generation have things in common, and they do. Because I was born at the very end of the Baby Boomer era, and because I identify more closely with the generational influences that came after that era, I call myself a Gen X. But it's important to note that these generational labels are fluid. In some families, the generations might be aligned as follows: 1960, 1980, 2000, 2020, but others might align differently, such as 1970, 1990, 2010. The twenty years of a generation is also not exact. While these things include a lot of variability, the broad groupings have been constructed because the people born during these times do indeed share similar attributes.

The reason they share similar attributes is this: *we are all a product of the external influences that were prevalent as we grew up.* Therefore, people growing up in the 1960s and 1970s are influenced by the themes and world events that were significant at that time. Those things that they see, those formative experiences, are what form the ideals and the values of the people in those generations.

That is why we're able to draw these very broad groupings of people when the only thing they have in common is that they happen to be born in the same twenty-year period, give or take. What they have in common is what was going on in the world, what they remember when they grew up, and these are their formative experiences.

Somebody who was a Baby Boomer and who grew up in the 1970s might remember when man first walked on the moon. For them, one of the exciting things that happened in their lifetime was the space race. Associated with this is the Cold War because the race between the US and Russia to get to the moon or to explore space was a manifestation of the struggle between the two countries. So, the Cold War was also an important thing for them.

Now, contrast this with someone from the Traditionalist generation who actually lived through war times or who might've been drafted and fought in World War II and saw the conflict between countries that led to that world war and the immense destruction from that world war. They would have a very different perspective on war itself than their children.

This example illustrates *why* we can label generations. The values of people in any generation are driven by their influences when growing up, and their influences growing up will be similar to the influences of other people who grew up around the same time.

At the end of the day, they are generalizations, which means they don't apply to everybody. Not every Baby Boomer thinks like this, rather everybody is a product of their own nature and nurture, and for a lot of Baby Boomers, they have a lot of those influences in common, and that leads to particular attributes or values that they might display.

Given that there are many differences *within* a generational label, new labels are now being created that are no longer based on when a person was born, but on knowledge and abilities that bring groups together. One example is Generation C, which represents people of all ages who have a strong understanding of technology. We'll discuss this further in a later chapter.

Nature versus Nurture

Our children are not replicas of ourselves. If we look at generation gaps, you have two conflicting things at play: nature and nurture. This is a long-standing debate: what is the greater influence on a person, nature or nurture? In "Why Nature & Nurture Won't Go Away," Steven Pinker states that "People's beliefs about the relative importance of heredity and environment affect their opinions on an astonishing range of topics . . . With so much seemingly at stake in so many fields, it is no surprise that debates over nature and nurture evoke more rancor than just about any issue in the world of ideas."[6] This debate has been going on for hundreds of years and will continue to go on forever.

The answer to this debate is not a simple one or the other. Both have a degree of influence, and the debate becomes about the specifics of *how* each one influences us. An interesting aspect of this issue is looking at when those two influences can conflict. As children, we inherited certain genetic material from our parents, and therefore, in some ways, we're similar to our parents. That is nature. We might've grown up in a home that was our parents' home that embodied their values. That's what we have in common with our parents.

What we do *not* have in common with our parents are the influences from outside. That's nurture. Nurture has two components: the nurturing that happens in the home and the nurturing that happens from external things that we experience.

It's that second component of nurture that drives generation gaps because the reason we can label generations is that each

6 Pinker, Steven. "Why nature & nurture won't go away." *Daedalus* 133.4 (2004): 5–17.

generation is a product of the influences that they grew up with. Those influences that occur in our formative years are very different.

The Generation Gap

The best example of a generation gap is the internet. Baby Boomers grew up without the internet, but their children and grandchildren grew up in a world never knowing that there wasn't such a thing as the internet. This influences how they communicate with each other.

Baby Boomers tend to prefer face-to-face or telephone communication. On the other hand, their children and grandchildren look at those methods of communication as archaic and anachronistic. Why talk to somebody face-to-face when you can SMS or WhatsApp them? Besides communicating differently, they look at the process of interpersonal communication in a completely different manner.

Communication is complex. It comprises three basic elements: words, modality (the way we say the words), and the nonverbal (like body language). The people from the generation who are more strongly influenced by face-to-face communication would see the full richness of that as a form of communication. On the other hand, their children and grandchildren might be able to get fully complete communication experience just from chat and emojis (which in some way, 'replace' modality and nonverbal).

Another example relates to a generation's perspective on the world. A Baby Boomer might've grown up influenced by the Cold War and the Civil Rights Movement of the 1960s, the assassination of leaders, such as John F. Kennedy and Martin Luther King. On the other hand, their children and grandchildren, who have not been drafted, have not lived through a depression, are living in a world that doesn't appear to be threatened by war.

The threats to the world that Baby Boomers saw were military threats of war. That is not a threat that a Millennial has ever seen. They look at war and they do not believe that it is going to threaten the destruction of the world. Instead, what is going to threaten the destruction of the world, according to them, might be climate change, because that is, in their formative years, what they saw as the greatest threat to the world. Therefore, they will place a higher value on the environment and preserving it.

On the other hand, their parents may place a higher value on having a strong military. Their children might say, "Why the hell do you need a military? There's no risk," but their parents' views were formed by seeing what war can do to the world on a large scale. Their children never saw it; therefore, it's not important to them. It's those things that are the drivers of generation gaps.

Generation gaps will always exist. Anybody who is old now was once young and with older parents. The reason generation gaps always exist is because the world is changing and people will always be growing up with different influences by what's around them, and that will drive their values. Therefore, their values will be different in some way from another generation.

Generational Challenges & Opportunities

When we look back at previous generations, we often think about the opportunities they had. Some people think about those who were around after World War II and say to themselves, "Wow, what a fantastic time of opportunity. There will never be a time like that again. Those people happened to live in that time, and they had a unique opportunity nobody else had. What chance do I have?" I disagree with that proposition because every generation has its own challenges and its own opportunities. The opportunities that existed then may not exist now, but new opportunities do exist. What we need to do is identify them and live within our present, rather than live in somebody else's past.

No one generation has more opportunity than another. Baby Boomers had a unique set of opportunities. Millennials grew up with technology throughout their lives, and that allowed them to access more information and connect with more people from throughout the world.

One of my customers was telling me about the early days of his online food ordering business. When he started the business, using Google Adwords, it cost him $1 to acquire a customer. After that customer's very first use of service, they received about $4 profit. The customer's lifetime value was actually far greater than that because after they used the service once, they were more likely to use it again, and continue to use it. He launched a new business last year, having sold this one for $850 million dollars, and he said that now it costs him $8 to acquire a customer, where they only get a $4 return after the first use. They don't even break even on the customer acquisition cost until the customer has made a second purchase, and they don't even know if the customer will ever use it again. You could look at this example and think: when he started that business, that was a unique opportunity when Google Adwords were priced such that he could reach critical mass faster while spending less money, and that window of opportunity isn't available anymore.

In a way, that's correct. That particular method of acquiring customers with those specific economics existed five to seven years ago and do not exist now. They've been replaced by different economics. On the flip side, he no longer has to introduce the idea of ordering online to people, which he had to do then. What came with the industry five to seven years ago were some barriers he had to overcome that don't have to be overcome now.

You can't copy someone else's success (because the context will always be different), but you can learn from their mistakes what to avoid. Every generation, and even within generations every few years, opportunities come and go and barriers come and go. It's best not to mull over what was and why it's not there or bemoan it, but rather, look at what is now. Look at the challenges you face now and the opportunities that you face now.

Bridging Generation Gaps in Communication

So how to bridge these gaps? Rather than everybody going out of their way to know what everybody else should and shouldn't know, just be aware that somebody doesn't necessarily speak the same language as you. If you were speaking with a person who has a different first language, you'd be tolerant of somebody who doesn't speak English well. In the same way, when speaking inter-generationally, you have to be tolerant of people who use different expressions or who don't know the meaning of expressions that you use that are second nature to you.

To ask a Millennial to be aware of the terms that are in common usage for them, that they grew up with, but that mean nothing to somebody else, like to a Gen X, is asking too much. Rather, what you each have to do is be tolerant. Be patient when somebody says, "What the hell does that mean?" If you say, "WTF," be prepared for somebody else to not even know what WTF means.

What I'm preaching is tolerance more than anything. Recognize differences, but don't feel obliged to jump through hoops not to offend people (which might be termed "political correctness"). If I'm going to be dealing with a Baby Boomer, I do not have to learn all of their terms and go through my entire vocab and say, "Oh, they don't know what that means, they don't know what that means." I'll say what I'm going to say. I might say to them at the start of the conversation, "If I'm using a word that you're not familiar with, by all means, let me know and I'll explain it to you." That's just tolerance. Tolerance for differences in communication is essential.

Understanding Generational Labels Action Step

Go to your *Transition Workbook* and follow along with the Understanding Generational Labels exercises. Take a few minutes to reflect on the events in your life that have impacted and influenced you. Go further by learning about the events that have influenced other generations. To download your complimentary workbook, go to www.DavidWerdiger.com/transition-workbook

CHAPTER 2

Creating a Legacy for You and Your Business

"What you do is your history. What you set in motion is your legacy."
– Leonard Sweet

You are Part of Something Much Greater

Why do people want to create a legacy? A legacy gives a person immortality. We're all born and we all die; nobody has yet found out a way to cheat that system. However, families are something that transcend an individual and can endure for many generations. A family legacy is something that is bigger than a nuclear family—bigger than an individual. That is why it's attractive; it gives us something that lives on, that we can live on through. That is why family legacy is so important to many people.

Sporting clubs are a lot like families: they endure, they have their ups and downs, they're competitive, they have culture, and they have spirit. They have all the elements of families, and they welcome players and fans into them like family members. The bond between a fan and their team is something that is very strong, that is something that they often want to pass onto their children. If I'm a Giants fan, then my children are going to be Giants fans, and we're not even going to talk about the Jets in the family.

Sporting clubs have legacies and dynasties. People talk about the dynasty of the New England Patriots. While dynasties are remembered by the personalities and the key people along the way that made them happen, they're all part of a team. The reason I'm such a big NFL fan (despite living in Australia) is because it is a sport that depends so much on teamwork. A "champion team" in NFL will always beat a "team of champions." In American football, it starts with the offensive and defensive lines. A team may have the best quarterback in the world, but if he is put behind a weak offensive line, then he'll get hurried and sacked. The game flows outwards from those lines; everybody has to do their job. If everybody fulfills their assignments, then anybody can come into the system, learn it, and be successful. This is the key to the Patriots' success; their system is so good and well taught that they are able to bring otherwise "ordinary" players into it and make them better for it.

This is the power of teamwork. Sporting dynasties like this can go on for several years of sustained success. It's done because the team is all working together toward a common goal and all leveraging their strengths and the strengths of others. They all know what role they have to play as part of the bigger team. They'll do whatever it takes for the betterment of the team, because it's not about the individual, it's about the team. Families have to strike that balance between the personal and the family because just like a team, it is composed of individuals who are part of the family, but no individual is greater than a family, and the family is more than the sum of its members.

Storytelling

A legacy is made up of the values that you transmit from one generation to another and that continue to be transmitted across many generations. How do you create a legacy? By telling stories. Ancient cultures transmitted knowledge and values through storytelling. Generations share wisdom by telling stories about what they experienced and what they learned from those experiences. Those stories can be of success and they can be of failure, but those stories are the most powerful instruments of transmitting culture.

One of the most celebrated Jewish festivals is Passover, which celebrates the Exodus of the Jews from Egypt. The original event that we mark happened about three and a half thousand years ago, and yet every year, Jewish families get together to celebrate this event. Entire families come together, often several generations in the same room, and they retell the story of the Exodus. As a social construct, this is an extremely powerful transmission of a legacy. It celebrates the formation of the Jewish nation, and it does so:

- through storytelling,
- over a family meal, which often stretches for many hours, and
- with multiple generations present.

The imperative associated with this meal, which is known as a Seder,[7] is the biblical injunction (Exodus 13:8), "And you should tell your child." This is an example of how to maintain a legacy—

7 "Passover Seder." *Wikipedia.* Wikimedia Foundation.

by gathering together multiple generations and telling stories on a regular basis. Those stories are the way the family legacy is maintained and transmitted from one generation to another.

We remember things, and when we start to forget things, we construct a story to help us remember them; they become a story. As The Doctor wisely observed in the classic sci-fi show *Doctor Who*, "Stories are where memories go when they're forgotten." Obviously, as each generation passes, the story will get changed and altered, but that doesn't matter because what the story does is transmit a message. The details become less important than the underlying message, the values and the legacy, that the story seeks to transmit.

This is how families can transmit their values and maintain a legacy through telling stories. It's a tried and proven method in cultures around the world that have been around for thousands of years; the way they maintain themselves is through a strong storytelling culture. One can see this in ancient cultures like the Aboriginal Australians and Native Americans. The messages that get transmitted are the stories we choose to tell.

It's much the same in companies; they too use storytelling as a way to transmit the corporate culture. The companies that are selective in their storytelling and pretend that bad things never happened are making a huge mistake because what happened, happened. You don't have to *celebrate* the bad things, but if you want people to remember them and most importantly to learn from them, then you must keep transmitting them, while at the same time looking forward.

A three-generation family business that I counsel maintains a gallery in their corporate office of stories going back to the founder in the early 1900s and his struggles to get the company started. The stories have been documented, with pictures where possible. Family members and employees are invited to contribute to the collection, and every year another story is chosen and added to the gallery. Employees are welcome to visit and spend time in the gallery, and all senior managers are taken on a tour by a family member as part of their induction into a management position.

Family Business versus Your Own Dreams

The family business is often the dream of the business founder, but it is not necessarily the dream of the business founder's children, grandchildren, or great-grandchildren.

Family members don't often choose to join the family business. In some family businesses, it is expected. One of the oldest family businesses in the world is a little B & B in Japan that's been going for forty-five generations since around the year 700.[8] What happens if the "number one son" turns eighteen and does not want to join the business? His father, grandfather, and his great-grandfather all joined the business when they turned eighteen. Now it is his turn, but he wants to travel the world. The business is profitable. He feels that it doesn't really need him. He has other dreams.

We all have our own dreams. But when it comes to family businesses, sometimes children don't have that choice. It is expected of them, and they go along with the family expectations of others, that one day all this will be theirs. The children find themselves working in a business that is not theirs. It is not of their own making. It is not their own dreams.

8 "The World's Oldest Family Companies." *Family Business—The World's Oldest Family Companies.* Web.

James E. Hughes Jr., author of *Family Wealth: Keeping it in the Family,* is concerned that instead of creating our own dreams, we are "stewarding someone else's dream." We have a notion of owners of a business, or directors of a business, being custodians. It is their job to act in the interests of shareholders. That is the fiduciary responsibility, but are they finding that experience fulfilling? If they are being rewarded appropriately, then it is a job, but if it is a family business, it is more than just a job. It's the *family business.*

We have a life—one that starts and finishes. If we have children, then we can pass on something to our children. At some point, our time on this world will cease, and hopefully our children will outlive us. A family business is something completely different. A family business is something that outlives people. When people are born into a multi-generational family business, it is the continuation of somebody else's dream.

Like a legacy, it is a way to become immortal because a family business can outlive many, many generations. You can look back five, six, seven generations to the founder, like this one in Japan, forty-five generations to the founder of the business, and all of those people's descendants may be living the founder's dream, instead of their own dream. Everyone has their own lives and their own passions. The challenge in any family business, as new people come into the business, is to ensure that they are indeed living their own lives.

While it might have been the dream of their grandfather that family members are employed in this business, it may not be the dream of their grandchildren. For the grandfather, it was the family store. For the father, it was the family retail chain. Their grandchildren may look at the business completely differently. They might feel that the business provides lifestyle and liquidity, but they do not have an emotional attachment to the business itself the way their ancestors did. The younger generation may just want to hire a manager and let them run it.

This is the challenge for any family business, particularly for new people coming into it. It is a challenge to make sure that new family members who are coming into the family businesses are using it as a way to live their own dreams, rather than being custodians of somebody else's dream. If that means their role is different, then so be it.

Accordingly, the family business has to evolve to allow them to fulfill their own dreams. That is something that the custodians of the family business should consider. How can the business evolve to meet a new generation of needs and also a new generation of dreams?

Connecting Generations through Shared Values

As I've discussed, there are differences between generations, but at the same time, people from different generations have things in common. Families will evolve as new family members come in and take a more active role in the family business, but there will be some values that they can use to connect between generations. Families shouldn't always be focusing on how they're different. Generations are different in any family, but they also have things in common in any family. That's something that families need to look for. In the first chapter of your *Transition Workbook,* you looked at what your influences are and how they shape your values. That is something that highlights generational *differences.* Families also need to focus on what brings them together. What is your family legacy? What are the values that you want to see endure from one generation to the next?

This is finding balance between the individual and the family, the balance between individual values and influences that change from one generation to the next, and family values that you want to persist from one generation to the next.

Creating a Legacy for You and Your Business
Action Step

Go to your *Transition Workbook* and follow along with the Creating a Legacy for You and Your Business exercises. Take some time to envision your legacy and the values you hope to pass down to future generations. To download your complimentary workbook, go to www.DavidWerdiger.com/transition-workbook

CHAPTER 3

Identity and Values in Business

"When your values are clear to you,
making decisions becomes easier."
– Roy E. Disney

The Relationship between You and Your Business

People have multiple identities and multiple roles that they play in their lives. Business owners have a type of relationship with their businesses. It is important that those roles are congruent, that our multiple roles are internally consistent with whatever and whoever we are.

Many years ago, a business coach I worked with pressed home the message of being honest with yourself. She asked me about when I was dishonest or broke the law. My instinctive response was that I am an honest, law abiding citizen. She challenged that statement and wanted me to reflect more closely on my actions.

When asked if I ever speed, I nodded yes. My initial response was to rationalize; all the other cars were going at the same speed, but then I thought more about it, "Yes, you are right. I am breaking the law, and I'm very aware that I'm breaking the law in that way."

I might be less comfortable breaking the law in other ways, but if the speed limit is thirty-five, and I'm going forty-five, I'm comfortable breaking the law. The discussion raised my awareness that every time I speed, I am indeed breaking the law. I wouldn't break the law in business. I wouldn't steal something from somebody, yet I'm prepared to break the law every time I go over the speed limit. When viewed in that way, I'm actually being inconsistent: some laws are OK to break, but not others.

While people may not always be totally consistent, there are certain core values that we can maintain throughout our different roles. What are your personal values? One of my personal values is helping others; I enjoy it, and it's an important part of who I am.

Identifying this aspect of myself was an "ah-ha" moment that caused me to look more broadly at my path in life and in business. The business I had built was an *enabler* business—we created billing software for phone companies. Looking deeper, this was essentially about *helping* emerging phone companies launch by pricing our service in such a way that it was attractive for start-up companies.

The business that I had created was actually an embodiment of my personal values. Many people who start up businesses may do this subconsciously. I suddenly realized that I love to help people, and I had chosen to do things outside of my personal life that supported these values.

I think this ends up happening more often than not because, as a leader of a business, you are an individual. People around you see you and see what your values are because you express your values through what you do and how you deal with others. Therefore, it stands to reason that the business that you create is, in some way, an embodiment of your personal values.

Some people have a dissonance of values between themselves and their business. They might be very unethical, immoral, or even illegal in their business practices. However, when it comes to their family, they might be the nicest person in the world: they would never dream of doing anything to hurt their family. When they go to work, suddenly they put on a completely different face—a completely different persona—and they turn into a corporate psychopath. While that is an extreme case, it's certainly a well-known phenomenon. In that case, there is a dissonance of values. They have one set of values for one role and another set of values for another role. Which are their *true* values? It can be hard to tell. Do they even know themselves? Whatever the case, that is not a good situation for anyone to be in. It is important to take some time to really identify and apply your own personal values to your business and your life.

Business Boundaries

What is your business for? Sometimes, people who own businesses have a lot of trouble drawing a line between themselves and their business—between their regular day-to-day personal life and their business life. This is particularly true for people who start their business and work from home or are in business with family members or with their spouse. Because home is both where they live and the workplace, or because they have both a personal and business relationship with a family member, drawing a clear line separating the two can be challenging.

In cases like that, the line between their personal life and their business life becomes blurry. A friend of mine left a corporate job and went into business with his wife. The concept didn't make sense to me. I go to my office in the morning, and then I come home at the end of the day (yes, I do some work from home, but it's not excessive). One of the benefits of this is that work gives me my own personal space.

It's very important to have boundaries between your personal roles and your business roles, so they don't bleed over and adversely affect each other. It is not healthy to bring your work life home with you. If you had a tough day at work, it is not fair to your personal relationships to bring that home. They did not contribute to whatever happened at work, so they ought not to have to bear any consequences of it. For the sake of your mental health and your personal relationships, it helps to learn how to compartmentalize. Make sure that your business and you stay separate, even though they do embody the same values.

When starting with a blank slate, it is a lot easier to create and form a business in your image. You can clearly establish these kinds of boundaries from the beginning. However, if you are already in a family business, and you want to make the sorts of boundary changes I've discussed, it is still possible. The first step is to identify the people with whom you have a business relationship and those with whom you have a personal relationship. For some, you may have both.

If those relationships are bleeding across into each other or adversely impacting each other, the key thing to do is go back to the negotiating table with those people. The fact that you may never have formally negotiated the terms of the relationship in the past is of no consequence. The meeting agenda is to establish an agreement on a new way of working together, moving forward. You need to sit down, negotiate it, and possibly even document it. For example, one agreement could be, "From such and such a date forward, we will no longer do this at work and we will no longer do this at home, or in interactions outside the workplace." Reach that accord with those people and find a way through that process, to have a separation, to pull apart two roles that were too tightly joined together, or had poorly defined boundaries.

If a couple in a relationship is working in a business together, they see each other all day long. They have to come up with some solution so that they can separate the business from their personal life. They may come to an agreement that between certain hours of the day, they are not allowed to talk about business, *no matter what.* For example, my wife and I have an agreement that in the bedroom, we don't talk about financial matters. This is a long-standing agreement that we made explicitly, early in our marriage. There are two options to resolve a situation where the topic comes up: either defer the discussion or leave the bedroom and discuss it elsewhere.

This agreement is about creating *spaces.* Those spaces can be physical spaces, times of the day, or times of the week that are sacrosanct. You simply do not do certain things during those times or in those places. It is something that has to be done very consciously. It is hard to let these things naturally evolve because they won't. They were already in a particular state, so you have to go through a process to unwind them, to pull them apart. It's like pushing a reset button.

Establishing Your Goals

The first step is to identify these two roles—you, the person, and you, the business owner—and then identify your personal values and business values. If they converge, look at how. The values that are in common between you and your business are obviously very important values to you. If there is a dissonance between your personal values and business values, you need to ask yourself why that is the case, how the dissonance can play out in practice and determine what, if anything, should change.

L-3 Triangle—Lifestyle, Liquidity & Leadership

The L-3 Triangle is something that I developed together with the CEO of my business. This was at a stage when the business I had created was already mature, and we reached a fork in the road in the business. I had decided several years earlier that I would take progressively small steps back from the operational side of the business, and focus more on the strategic. The path was going well, but it came to this juncture because my relationship with the general manager at the time had become dysfunctional. In hindsight, this was exactly because we didn't have a clear demarcation of our respective roles in the business, and were regularly stepping on each other's toes. I had two opposite pieces of advice from two experienced people I respected: either sack the manager and revert to a more hands-on role in managing or take a big step back from the business. I chose the latter.

That big step back was very important for me as an individual, and included the establishment of an advisory board in my business. The previous general manager moved on, and a new CEO, who had previously worked in the business, took her place. That new structure allowed me to have a much clearer delegation of authority in the business. I was 100% owner and remained fully invested in and committed to the business. The business was very important to me. I was as passionate about the business as before, but I recognized that the business now needed me in a different role.

When you create a business, it is like a child. You give birth to a child, and the child grows up and needs different things from you as a parent, at different stages in the child's life. A business, in its infancy, needs you to attend to it 24/7 and tend closely to its every need. Then the business grows up and starts to be a little bit more independent, and it needs different things from you as a "parent."

Eventually (hopefully), the business grows into adulthood. As an adult business, it does not need to be smothered anymore by a parent. On the contrary, just like a child can suffer from being emotionally smothered by their parents, a business suffers from being smothered by its owners. Sting once said, "If you love someone, set them free." If you love a business that you have created, then at some point, you need to set it free and let it be its own business—let it have its own identity. That identity will be strongly influenced by you because you created it, but eventually, it has its own identity, and you have to be open to letting it have that identity.

The incoming CEO asked me what I wanted from the business. We spent many hours over a number of weeks trying to get a clear picture of the delegation from ownership to management. When ownership and management are tightly enmeshed, it is very hard to articulate the distinctions. By separating myself operationally from that business, setting up an advisory board, and having a clear separation of powers, I was still 100% owner, but I was formally delegating management of the business on a day-to-day basis to the CEO.

We developed what we called the *L-3 Triangle*, which represented the three things that I wanted from my business. Some of these are things that you may also want from your business. You might have your own L-3 Triangle, or you might have an M-4 Square.

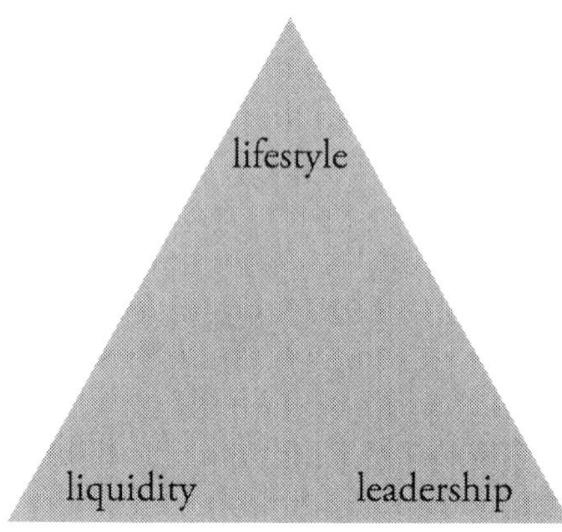

Lifestyle—The business needs to meet my lifestyle. I will not be a slave to the business. I choose to work a set number of hours or whatever the business needs from me in my particular role at the time. In this way, the business facilitates my doing whatever I need or want to do with the rest of my time. That might be other businesses I have created, or it might be pursuing other interests entirely. The point is that I am free to choose.

Liquidity—The business needs to be profitable. It needs to deliver a return on investment and a dividend to the owner. This is quite essential for any business owner. While any business needs initial investment and is not likely to be profitable from day one, ultimately the business needs to be profitable to the extent that it can return an appropriate dividend to its owners, and perhaps more.

Leadership—The business needs to be seen as a leader in its industry. I was doing some pioneering work in the telecommunications industry, and it was important for me to be recognized as a leader in what I do. That was a matter of personal pride because I had created something, and I wanted to be the best at it and acknowledged as such. I didn't need to win awards; rather I wanted the business to be known in the industry as really good at what we do.

Your Relationship with Your Business

At all times, it's important to have a good *relationship* between you and your business. What does that even mean? When we think of relationships, they are usually between individuals and between groups, not between a business owner and their business. There are two elements to this. Firstly, that you have sufficient emotional distance between you and your business. Secondly, that you are comfortable with you, the person in your regular life, and your business, as an entity separate from you. The purpose or mission of the business and your own purpose as an individual should be aligned.

Your business ought to be an asset. It is a business that is separate from you and has its own identity and value outside of you. Ask yourself if your business is delivering your lifestyle desires. If your lifestyle desire is to go to work every single day in your business, then doing that is contributing to meeting your lifestyle needs.

Is the business going to meet your lifestyle needs in five to ten years? If your lifestyle needs change, then your relationship with your business may need to change as well. You might be happy for the next five years, working sixty-hour weeks, but you should always be prepared for change. At some point, you are not going to want to do that anymore. Your lifestyle needs will change. You need to start preparing your business now to be able to meet your changing lifestyle needs, so don't be resistant to change.

If you have a business that currently depends on you working sixty hours a week, at some point, you might want to be able to walk away from that and just work twenty hours a week. That change is not going to happen overnight (unless there is a sudden and disruptive event in your life). That transition is a slow and painstaking process from two perspectives—from a business process perspective, because somebody is going to have to replace you, and equally from an emotional perspective.

If you are that deeply invested in your business and working that much in your business, then there are very few emotional barriers between you and your business. It's important to start building those boundaries between you and your business in order to separate from it and let it become the asset that you want it to be.

Start thinking about it now because you do not always know what is going to happen in the future. You can be running a business or working sixty hours a week, but then suddenly, something happens in your family and you can't work that amount of time anymore. You might be forced to cut down before you have the systems in place, and that puts your business at risk.

That is a part of risk mitigation in any business—the principle that everybody in a business should be replaceable, including you. That was what I learned from Michael Gerber's book *The E-myth Revisited*—that the value of a business is in its systems.[9] Things can

---

[9] Gerber, Michael E. *The E-myth Revisited: Why Most Small Businesses Don't Work and What to Do about It.* New York: Collins Business, 1995.

change for any number of reasons: it might be a lifestyle decision, an illness, or something else impacting your family.

In the early days of my business, customers would regularly comment to me, "This is all very good, but what if you were run over by a bus?" I didn't have an answer for them. If I were run over by a bus, I didn't know who would do their billing next month. It sure wouldn't be me. That is why it became very important to me, from a business continuity perspective, to ensure that I was not indispensable to my own business. As part of any risk mitigation strategy, you need to be able to replace any role. This is something that any business does. Doing this for employees and not for owners is a mistake. A business needs to do this for *everybody* who has a role in the business.

The Search for Balance

What if the family business conflicts with your own dreams? This begins the search for balance. People cannot always have it all. You can't necessarily have lifestyle, liquidity, and leadership. Assuming you couldn't have all three, which of them would you be prepared to give up? You do not necessarily have to give it all up completely, but you might need to adjust the balance and determine what one is the most important, what one is the second most important, and what is the third most important. Setting those priorities will drive future business and life decisions.

Your L-3 Triangle might not be an equilateral triangle; some sides of the triangle might be longer and others shorter, as a reflection of their relative importance. Liquidity may be more important to you; therefore, you might need to give up a bit on your lifestyle aspirations at the moment, so that there is more liquidity. From time to time, you might adjust them.

This becomes a search for balance because the things that are identified as your goals are not always fully aligned. Very often, they conflict with each other. Your own dreams may have to wait a little bit. You may need to focus on the family business and what it needs and give up a few of your own dreams. In a few years, after you have done what you need to do for the family business, then you will be able to put more emphasis on your own dreams.

The first step is to understand that sometimes they conflict; therefore, we have to prioritize some over the other. We have to search for that point where they are all in balance, and ultimately, find a plan to reach that point. The search for balance comes from a position of conflict. If we have different needs that conflict, then that gives rise to the need to find a balance between those conflicting goals.

Identity and Values in Business Action Step

Go to your *Transition Workbook* and follow along with the Identity and Values in Business exercises. Take some time to map your values and find balance between them. To download your complimentary workbook, go to www.DavidWerdiger.com/transition-workbook

CHAPTER 4

Entrepreneurs in the Family

"An entrepreneur isn't someone who owns a business, it's someone who makes things happen."

– Tim Ferriss

Entrepreneurs are a different breed of people, to the extent that there are two kinds of people—entrepreneurs and non-entrepreneurs. Entrepreneurs look at the world differently. They have something that other people don't have. Entrepreneurs are prepared to take a risk, and they have a creative side to them. Some entrepreneurs tend to look at the big picture rather than the details.

An entrepreneur will look at the world and see a business idea or have some solution to a problem that they want to turn into a venture. Often, that desire is bursting out and needs to be actualized; it needs to be put into practice in the form of a business venture. However, few meaningful ventures can be built and grown by just one person. Entrepreneurs, like most anybody, need to work with people that are very different from them. While many ventures need an entrepreneur to drive them, they also need all the other cogs in the wheel. Both entrepreneurs and non-entrepreneurs have to exist within a business for it to thrive and grow successfully.

Both types of people—entrepreneurs and non-entrepreneurs—need to understand each other. An entrepreneur might need investors. Those investors might be very dry and unforgiving of an entrepreneur, and may just be interested in a certain return on their investment. In any meaningful venture, it's not something that any one person can do alone. There are limits to what one person can do, especially if a business wants to scale. Because of that, entrepreneurs need to work with others, and the others, by necessity, need to be complementary to them.

If you look at the world a certain way, it can be difficult to learn to look at the world differently. However, what is not so difficult is to recognize that other people do look at the world differently. If you do that, then you can realize that they coming from a different place, and that is why they're saying whatever they are saying. You may not necessarily see it, but *they* see it, and you need to be able to live with that.

Even within the class of entrepreneurs, some people are more big-picture, some are more detail-focused, and others are able to switch between the two. Recognize that when you're working with other people, perhaps in partnerships with other entrepreneurs, one person might be detail-oriented and the other person big-picture. You need to be aware of those differences in learning how to work with other people.

Masters of Entrepreneurship

After I set up an advisory board for my business, it was important that I stepped back from the business, both operationally and emotionally, and this left me with a void. By this time, I was in my early forties, and it seemed like as good a time as ever to get an MBA. The challenge was it had been a long time since I'd done any formal university-type study.

I attended an MBA informational evening and learned about the course, but it just didn't click with me. Afterward, I spoke to the presenter about my concerns. I had never worked for large corporations and had no interest in climbing any corporate ladders, so an MBA did not seem to be the right fit. He recommended that instead, I consider a Masters of Entrepreneurship and Innovation (MEI), something that until then I never knew existed. His advice was insightful and relevant to me, and that is what I ended up doing. Due to "education inflation," MBAs and similar degrees are almost necessary to get a job these days.[10] The Masters of Entrepreneurship and Innovation felt a little more distinctive.

It turned out to be a fantastic experience for me. A number of my fellow students wondered why I was taking the course since I was already an entrepreneur. But for me, that was not a barrier to further learning. The opportunity to go back and study with the benefit of plenty of experience was in fact an opportunity to reflect on what I had achieved, what I hadn't achieved, and how I went about doing what I did. There are two possible approaches: one is to think about all of the things you should have done differently, but that is the wasteful path of regret. The better way is to learn from your experience, reflect on the decisions that you made and the path you took. If you choose to do it again, you'll be able to do it far

10 "any of a number of related processes involving increased demands for formal educational qualifications, and the devaluation of these qualifications. In Western society, there have been increasing requirements for formal qualifications or certification for jobs" "Credentialism and Educational Inflation." *Wikipedia.* Wikimedia Foundation. Web.

better with that knowledge.

The Entrepreneurial Spirit

Entrepreneurs have a desire to change things. They look at the world and want it to be different. They want to create things that aren't there already because they look at a problem and see a solution that other people don't see.

Recently, I was speaking to some high school students about my life. At the end, a student asked, "What inspires you?" I said, "I don't know, I just have this burning desire to share my ideas with the world in the hope that it makes people's lives better." That's part of the entrepreneurial spirit. An entrepreneur cannot just sit on their laurels and work a 9-to-5 job. They just won't be fulfilled from doing that.

Some people find it hard to understand that. They may be very happy with things the way they are and happy to work at a job day to day and have a regular life.

When Edmund Hillary was asked, "Why did you climb Mt. Everest?" he famously said, "Because it's there." Some people believe mountains are there to admire because they're beautiful things, and other people say mountains are there to be climbed. Non-entrepreneurs look at a mountain and say, "Wow, that's beautiful," and entrepreneurs say, "Wow, I must climb that. I need to surmount that goal." Entrepreneurs see goals that need to be achieved. Others see mountains or obstacles.

The world is changing very rapidly, and the business world is constantly moving forward. If we just sit still, then everything will move ahead of us. So if you are not also moving forward, then you are actually moving backward.

Time for another sports analogy. Teams are super-competitive and always looking for an edge in order to climb up the ladder in a competition. They need to improve at a faster rate than everybody else because *everybody* is improving. Just being better than last season isn't good enough—more importantly, it won't help achieve your goals

Willingness to Take Risks

I consider the entrepreneurial side of a person to be creative. Often people use the term entrepreneurship together with innovation. Innovation is from the word "novel"—new—it means to create a new way of doing something. Innovators look at the way people do things and find better ways to do them, to "build a better mousetrap." Entrepreneurship is related, but different. Entrepreneurship is about creating an enterprise, a venture, a business. This adds an element of risk-taking.

People who innovate or invent things are not necessarily taking any risk. Being prepared to do something when you don't have certainty of your future earning capability, not being paid regularly, and not working for somebody else—that is a core part of entrepreneurship. You are taking a leap and deciding that you want to do something, and you are prepared to risk the regular income stream associated with being an employee. Entrepreneurs are driven by the desire to create and to build an enterprise, a business. This desire to create is strong enough that they are prepared to take a risk.

It's not just about wanting to take risks for the thrill of it. Rather, it's about being prepared to take a risk *in order to create something.* That is the essence of the entrepreneurial spirit. That comes from many different emotional places, and there are a lot of ingredients. The appetite for risk is an important ingredient, but if you're somebody who just likes to take risks, that doesn't mean you will necessarily be an entrepreneur. On the other hand, if you are an entrepreneur, you do need to be prepared to take risks.

Non-entrepreneurs often view entrepreneurs in general as risk-*takers,* but that is not the case. The risk-taker is somebody who enjoys the ups and downs of taking risks in and of itself. For example, they might enjoy gambling—the thrill of putting it all on red or watching their horse competing. Entrepreneurs don't take risks for the sake of taking risks (like a gambler); rather, they take risks to achieve a certain goal. Their perspective is to take more *calculated* risks and to have far greater consideration for the downside than a gambler.

Good entrepreneurs are not risk-takers, but rather risk *managers.* They are able to understand and quantify the risks they're taking, not necessarily in a very formal way, but certainly quantify them to the extent that they know what risks they're taking and the (financial) return they can deliver.

Owning a Job versus Owning a Business

After completing university studies, I found a job, mostly because it was the obvious next thing to do in my life. Finish university (check), get a job (check), now start earning money (check). After a short amount of time, it became obvious to me that this was not the future for me. The future for me would be to be my own boss.

I wanted to be my own boss, not necessarily from the perspective of creating a business, but more from an autonomy perspective. I did not want to be accountable to others; I wanted to be the person in charge. I like the distinction between owning a job versus owning a business, which Robert Kiyosaki articulated well in his book *Rich Dad, Poor Dad.*[11] Very often the first step from having a job and being an employee is not to own a business, but rather to own a job—to move from employment to self-employment where you're working for yourself. You are your own boss, but you haven't necessarily created an enterprise out of it. All you've done is created a job for yourself.

That was my first step. As it started to move forward, I developed the view that I wanted to own a business. *Ultimately, I wanted the business to be something separate from me.* This is the difference between owning a job and owning a business. When you own a job, if you're not there, the job (and therefore the capacity for earning) is not there.

If you're a high-value professional, such as a doctor, you own a job if you're working for yourself. You may be paid a lot of money per consult or per hour, but as soon as you stop seeing patients, you stop earning money. On the other hand, if you own a business, the business has a life of its own, and you've created something (which includes an income stream) that exists without you. To me, that was actually the test of whether or not I had created something.

There are people who create a business, and the business is basically them. In that case, they are unable to sell it because the business has no value without them. They're the one who is earning all the money for the business. Now that doesn't mean the business isn't good. It may be very successful financially and deliver great cash flows. It may meet the needs of its owners. It's just that I didn't want a business like that. I wanted to go through all the steps: from having a job to owning a job, and then turning that job that I owned

---

11 Kiyosaki, Robert T., and Sharon L. Lechter. *Rich Dad, Poor Dad: What the Rich Teach Their Kids about Money—That the Poor and Middle Class Do Not!*

into a business was a logical progression.

I felt it was important to first have the experience of working at a job. That's probably important for most people because it does help you understand the other mindset. In the back of my mind, I had a long-term vision of owning a business, but I couldn't just dive in and start a business. Some people do. Some people do it when they're teenagers. At that stage in my life, I probably didn't have sufficient drive to just go ahead and do it myself without first experiencing the business world as an employee.

Entrepreneurs in a Family Business

Within a family environment, when you have someone who is an entrepreneur and you have another family member who doesn't have the entrepreneur mindset but they are involved together in a family business, it is especially important that they understand each other and be able to make sure that the business functions effectively.

Often, two siblings with very different personalities inherit, or become involved in, a family business. One might have more of an entrepreneurial perspective of things and the other one doesn't. There might be two children in a family business, where one has huge ambitions and the other one doesn't, or one looks at the business and sees what it can be and the other one just doesn't have that vision. At the same time, they are equally children. In many families, the value of equity among children (that they all have equal entitlements and are all treated equally) is very important.

It's about different people working together and recognizing their diversity and the different things that they bring to the business. Added to that, they happen to be related, which means they have to also consider how to juggle their personal relationship and be comfortable with the fact that they are equally children, but have different contributions to make to the family business.

Understand that somebody might have a different perspective from you. I can't imagine what it would be like to just be at a job and work 9-to-5 for somebody else. I did it for a period of time, but I could never do it again because the idea felt foreign to me. Even when I was working on a job, I worked extended hours because I just wanted to. However, I recognize that there are millions of people who do that every day, and they're fine with it, which means there must be some people who are comfortable with it. It's not me, but they're an important part of the business ecosystem. The business world can't run without them.

The world needs all different types of people, and the business world needs all different types of people. We gain more from diversity than from homogeneity. If everybody's the same, the world is a very boring place. Likewise, if everybody in a company is the same, it's a very boring place and actually a risky place as well. A company needs different voices and different perspectives so that it can be fully aware of any challenges it might face.

Two of my clients were brothers born just two years apart, but were chalk and cheese. The older one studied accounting and spent several years in a large firm. The younger one had entrepreneurship in his blood and started several micro-businesses in between *nearly* finishing a couple of university degrees. After they had each established their careers elsewhere, their father wanted to find roles for both of them in a large and diversified family business. The older one became Group CFO, with oversight over all of the subsidiary businesses, and reporting into the board. The younger one headed up diversified investments, building a private equity fund, and also continuing investment in startups where he could have a more active role. Both reported to the family board, which had two family members (aside from the brothers) plus three independents. This allowed each brother to have their autonomy and not step on each other's toes, and utilize their specific skills in support of the larger family enterprise.

In a family context, if there are multiple family members involved in the business, they all bring different things to the table. The fact that they happen to be tethered to the business by birth because they're family members is the reason for their commitment to the business or their equity in the business. That's very different from the contribution they can make to the business and what they bring as individuals.

A successful business needs all types of people. In a family business, there is always at least one entrepreneur (although they may no longer be in the business or even alive). Entrepreneurs have a unique way of approaching life and work as they strive to turn a solution into a venture. Alongside these entrepreneurs are the other members of the business who help to make it a reality. A successful business needs all types of people. For a smooth transition within your family business, understand and celebrate the strengths and contributions of entrepreneurs and non-entrepreneurs alike.

Understanding Entrepreneurs Action Step

Go to your *Transition Workbook* and follow along with the Understanding Entrepreneurs exercises. Take some time to identify your thoughts on entrepreneurs and how they have impacted your family business. To download your complimentary workbook, go to www.DavidWerdiger.com/transition-workbook

CHAPTER 5

Intergenerational Issues

"Intergenerational solidarity is not optional, but rather a basic question of justice, since the world we have received also belongs to those who will follow us."

– Pope Francis

As families shift from one generation to the next, individual and collective views regarding education, risk, and wealth also shift. Each generation grows up with different expectations and beliefs. The first generation of entrepreneurs has certain characteristics that bring them and their entrepreneurial ventures success. As the business moves into the second and third generations, there are many different paths it can take. Some paths lead to further success within the business; however, sometimes intergenerational issues lead to conflict and loss. This chapter will explore some of the common patterns and concerns among generations.

The Success of Immigrant Entrepreneurs

As part of my MEI degree, I undertook a project that sought to identify the underlying drivers of entrepreneurship, personally and in the surrounding culture and environment. Since I am child of a successful entrepreneur, a reasonable approach was to interview my father and two others to understand more deeply what it was about their immigrant experiences that influenced their success as entrepreneurs. Are there things about being an immigrant that helped them in their entrepreneurial pursuits? Are there things about overcoming adversity that make it more likely for someone to be able to be a successful entrepreneur? I asked them about their life and their journey, what motivated them, the effect of their hardship on their subsequent approach to life and how other factors like family, support structures, and beliefs affected their success.

There were a lot of commonalities between them. Each of the three of them had survived World War II and came to Australia afterward in search of a new life, having survived great adversity, having lost members of their family, and arriving here with almost no financial assets.

As you learned in Chapter 3, one of the qualities that drives entrepreneurship is the appetite for risk: an entrepreneur has to be prepared to take risks. They need to be willing to put a regular income at risk in order to build a business. All of these immigrants had gone through such terrible experiences that the thought of risking financial loss was nothing to them, relative to what they had already experienced. Their formative years had established an approach to risk that was different from most others. They had nearly died or been killed in the war; so what if they lose some money? It is not the worst thing in the world. They had experienced so much worse. Therefore, these immigrants already had, from their earlier experiences, one of the key ingredients to successful entrepreneurship—the appetite for risk.

There were also commonalities in regard to what they did with their money. All of these entrepreneurs created businesses in manufacturing and importing that were very successful and produced strong cash flows. That was a specific sector that was vibrant at the time. Importantly, rather than reinvest their profits in the business, they pulled them out and put them into hard assets, such as real estate. These were people who were displaced and were stateless at some time in their lives. They were taken away from their homes. Psychologically, in their new lives in a new country, they were drawn to the attraction of property as a store of wealth, as well as a vehicle for further wealth creation.

For hundreds of years, Jews in Europe traditionally purchased and held diamonds. The reason they did that is because it's a portable store of wealth. Because of their history of persecution, they needed to be prepared to move at any time. If they did, they had their wealth on them. They could just walk out the door if circumstances needed it and keep their wealth with them. But having established a new life in Australia, these immigrants felt more secure about their lives and wanted to bring back that sense of home and that sense of being tied to something.

In addition to these immigrant entrepreneurs being drawn to the importance of hard assets, family was also a way to rebuild the roots that they had lost through their experiences during the war. Again, they were putting a premium on the things that they missed out on. It was very important for them to make sure their children had the educational opportunities that they missed as children. In some cases, they put a very high value on a Jewish education as a driver of Jewish continuity. That led to a very strong Jewish education infrastructure and participation rates in Australia, far better than other places in the world.

The Baby Boomer generation was driven by a global phenomenon of people who experienced World War II, and perhaps also remembered World War I, and therefore, had a sense that the time of great wars was over. These immigrants, particularly Jewish immigrants who survived World War II, and in some cases the Holocaust, had a need to rebuild lost generations. It is a common Jewish tradition to name people after departed ancestors. They wanted to have large families to sustain and protect their culture and remember their lost relatives through their names.

Over time, their appetite for risk changed—it started to wane. When they came to Australia, they were hungry for success and had an appetite for risk. As they increased their wealth far beyond what they actually needed and grew older, they started to look forward to future generations and their needs, and their appetite for risk actually went down. They were no longer prepared to put their existing wealth at risk to the extent that they were before, in part because there was more of it to risk.

Intergenerational Lessons from Immigrant Entrepreneurs

When somebody immigrates, in a way, they are starting over. Often, they have come from a place that is culturally very different from where they are now. The circumstances of immigrant entrepreneurs and their families can give us some powerful insights into generational differences.

Looking at multi-generational American families, it can be easier to identify clear generational patterns. For example, in some families, the grandfather was in the military, the father was in the military, the son joined the military, and the grandson is going to join the military. Putting aside for a moment whether or not they want to, there is still a significant homogeneity between generations in such families. Despite the broader generational differences, they are all brought up in the same country, possibly in the same part of that country, and they all have that common occupation that is going down the family line. In the example above, each one is their own individual, but they share that military ethic.

Contrast that with the generational differences in the case of children of immigrants. Immigrants have come from a different country, from a different culture, and decided to make their lives or continue their lives in a new country and in a new culture. In the case of the immigrant entrepreneurs who have survived greater adversity, the differences between their previous lives and their current lives are even greater. Accordingly, immigrant entrepreneur families display a *far greater difference* between generations. It benefits us to learn from those families because, despite the differences, there are timeless lessons that they have learned, some of them informed by their experiences as immigrants or their adversity and some of them general lessons.

Attitudes to Partnerships

One thing that came through from these immigrants is that they always wanted to leave something for the other party in a partnership. They recognized that a partnership went two ways, and any partnership where one partner was doing significantly better than the other would lead to a situation where the other partner felt they weren't being well done by, and therefore, the potential for conflict. A successful partnership is where each partner is leaving something else for the other party as well.

Reputation

The other thing that was very interesting to these immigrants is the value of reputation. In business, the reputation they wanted was as somebody who people wanted to do business with. It was something intrinsically important to them; often their families in their birth countries had a particular standing within their communities and they, as the survivors of their family, had to take that with them and start it from scratch in a place where they were not known.

The other reason is more pragmatic. Why would you want your reputation to be as somebody people want to do business with? Because you want to be the person that others call when they want to do business. People do business with other people (rather than companies with companies), and therefore want to do business with others with whom they can get along.

I think the attitudes toward partnerships and reputation stem from the values they were brought up with at home. The ideas about partnerships stem from a sense of equity and justice. In addition, Jewish communal life places a high value on personal and family reputation.

Diversification

The other key lesson that these immigrants took with them is on diversification. They didn't believe that things could continue as they were forever. Investors often make this mistake: they reason that if the market is going up, it's going to keep going up forever. But the fact is that while markets have ups and downs, stockbrokers and traders seem to have the shortest memories of all people. Having lived through good times in their home country and then seeing them go bad was likely a strong and enduring lesson which formed their attitudes about what is going on around them. As a result, they didn't think that just because business is good now, something won't happen. It may not be as cataclysmic as they had experienced, but they maintained a vigilance and awareness of potential downside.

In their cases, the immigrants I interviewed turned out to be correct. They were all in the manufacturing business, and structural changes meant that manufacturing in Australia became less viable. Therefore, they hedged and rather than reinvesting to grow their businesses larger still, they diversified to the extent they were able to close down their original businesses and continue generating wealth using other assets. The attractive asset to them was commercial property, and as mentioned, to an immigrant who was forced to leave their home, the attraction to more secure assets like property made sense.

Self-Belief

They had a strong self-belief and the desire for self-improvement. You need self-belief to survive any adversity, and they had it in abundance, which probably contributed to their survival in the first place. This research project had inherent selection bias: the subjects had already survived and were all successful. Often, they thought and acted bigger than they were, which I found quite inspiring.

Networking

The biggest thing they've learned is that they don't exist as an island; they came to a country all alone but realized very quickly that they couldn't do it alone. For them, having a family and relationships was very important because it gave them the stability and the drive for something to live for. They valued networking as people who were building connections from scratch, who came to a new country as adults and really had to start again, unlike people born in a city who can build and network from a young age in their home city or in their home country.

The Education Pattern

There is an interesting multi-generational pattern among families of immigrant entrepreneurs—an oscillating effect that switches between generations. In the first generation, an immigrant comes to a new country. In their country of birth, he or she was deprived of an education, and despite that, overcomes great adversity, moves to a new country, and is very successful.

Parents often prioritize for their children the opportunities that they missed out on. The immigrant entrepreneur recognizes that he never received a formal education. To make up for that, he ensures his children—the second generation—have the best education possible. This leads the children on a career path of highly paid professionals, such as doctors, lawyers, or accountants. They take a different path because their path is driven by the opportunities that their education opens to them.

Once the children have established careers, they start comparing themselves to their parents and begin to wonder why they focused so much on their education. Yes, they are well-paid professionals, but they often do not make as much money as their entrepreneurial parents. Then their children—the third generation—see this and realize that their grandfather got by without an education and despite this managed to create a successful business. Their father is a high paid lawyer, who works sixty hours a week and never has a holiday. Once they make this comparison, they ask themselves, "What would I rather be?"

Each generation looks at the previous generation and the one before it and chooses. One says, "No, I'd rather go into business, and I don't think an education is needed." The other one says, "No, you missed out on an education. You need to have one." This develops into a pattern that has been observed throughout many different cultures and generations.

Family Wealth over Generations

Some entrepreneurs get so caught up in wild ride and end up losing their wealth, while others remain grounded. There are some entrepreneurs who create great wealth and become very tied up in the trappings of wealth, living a very extravagant lifestyle, and continue wanting to take risks. In the case of immigrants, this happens less often because they are more likely to retain a bit of humility of their earlier life. Perhaps that keeps them a bit more grounded than other high flyers.

Second Generation

Second generation immigrants—the first generation born in a new country—are very different from their parents. Depending on when they were born, what stage their parents were in their wealth creation, they may have little or no memory of their parents struggling and going through the process of creating wealth. As mentioned earlier, my elder siblings have memories of our family before we had wealth, but I don't.

My parents chose very deliberately not to flaunt their wealth—to remain very grounded because they didn't want to spoil us. Some of our friends and acquaintances who had also done very well lived far more extravagant lifestyles. My parents insisted on maintaining a very modest lifestyle. We were comfortable, and we were never short of anything, which in and of itself was a blessing.

Second generation immigrants sometimes struggle with being entrepreneurs. The second generation of an immigrant entrepreneur is someone who is brought up with everything they need and all the opportunities that their parents didn't have. The question is, do they want to be entrepreneurs or not? Herein lies the paradox: adversity is sometimes a good thing. Adversity creates a hunger. It makes a person want more. It is more difficult for somebody who is brought up with wealth to hunger for even more. If you are comfortable, you tend to have less ambition for more because you have everything you need.

Parents generally want their children to be as or more successful than them. This is what can pull the second generation in the other direction. A child of a high achiever wants to individuate and achieve something themselves, not just be the child of somebody else who has done well. This logic also applies to second generation entrepreneurs in general. There is an intrinsic need in everybody to be their own person and to not just be the son of somebody else successful.

With two paths before you, one which is the opportunity to get a high paid career through education and another one to be an entrepreneur and to not get paid until you create a business and make something, the lower-risk path is that of the professional. That is something that the second generation was often encouraged to do because the earlier generation didn't have the choice. The second generation has the choice. It is a difficult choice to decide to put the family money at risk or personal money at risk in order to create something and do something when you don't need to. What is driving the desire to that a risk?

The drive is unlikely to be purely the need to create material wealth. The people who are less financially stable are driven to take risks by the need to be more comfortable. That is less present in children of entrepreneurs. They don't need it; therefore, there must be something else in them that is driving them to take the entrepreneurial path.

What could that be? It could be that creative instinct inside them, the desire to create and build rather than just be part of a big engine working for somebody else. It could be the desire to individuate, to be their own person, not just to be somebody who is the child of another successful entrepreneur.

In summary, the second generation immigrant and the second generation entrepreneur have a very different pathway financially and emotionally toward becoming entrepreneurs. They are driven by different motivations than their parents.

Third Generation

"Shirtsleeves to shirtsleeves in three generations" is an old proverb that warns of the ups and downs of multi-generational family wealth. This proverb exists in many cultures—both Western and non-Western—and its origin is unknown. The Scottish express it well: "The father buys, the son builds, the grandchild sells, and his son begs." It neatly articulates the challenge for people in subsequent generations. There are private wealth organizations and professional consultancies dedicated to helping their members and clients retain the family wealth.

It seems counterintuitive: surely, it's harder to make it than to just hold on to it.

Nevertheless, we have seen that the third generation ends up losing the family wealth. It is important that the third generation is given the proper tools, education, and guidance in order to minimize the risk of this happening. The second generation may not remember a time when the first generation had not yet made money, but they have more tangible memories of the culture of wealth that the first generation established. The third generation, on the other hand, has even less of that. They are often brought up in even more luxury and trappings of wealth and therefore may have even less desire to do something with their lives. They are further separated from the first generation.

Let's consider the different roads the family wealth can travel through generations.

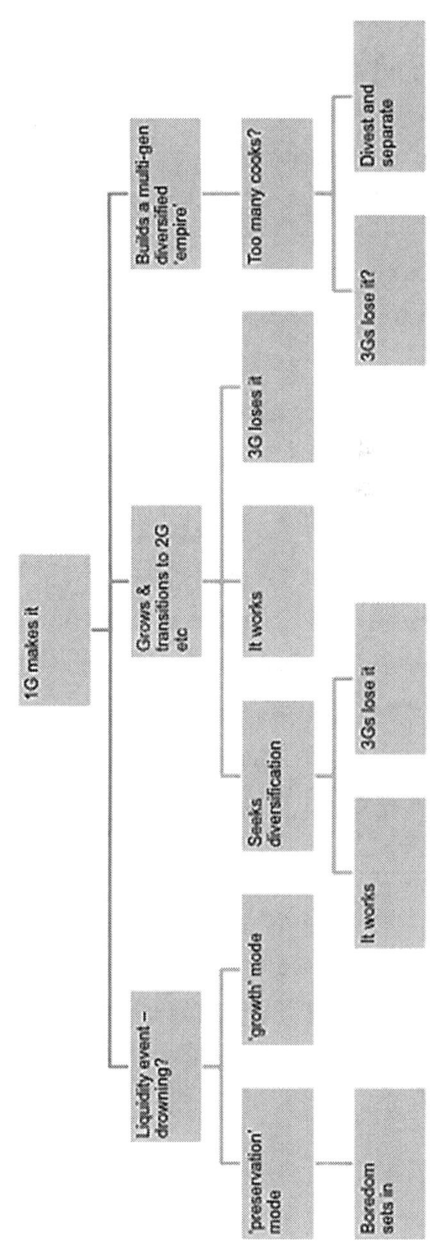
Changing Risk Appetites
1G makes it
Liquidity event – drowning?
Grows & transitions to 2G etc
Builds a multi-gen diversified 'empire'
'preservation' mode
'growth' mode
Seeks diversification
It works
3G loses it
Too many cooks?
Boredom sets in
It works
3Gs lose it
3Gs lose it?
Divest and separate

It all starts with the "1G" creating wealth. This is generally followed by three possible paths. They might have a liquidity event—a sale of the business. Suddenly, there is a gap. What does one do the morning after selling a business and taking a huge amount of cash off the table? As one person said to me, "Liquidity is a good thing, but sometimes you can drown in it." Families might go into preservation mode. They might want to talk to a private manager and invest it very conservatively and make sure they protect it and never lose it.

A liquidity event is a huge change for a family because their investment profile takes a huge shift. Previously, a significant part of their wealth was exposed to the family business. Now, it is in cash, and they have to start all over again with very different investment strategies than what they did before. Even if they had part of their wealth invested in a mix of passive investments, now there is much more, and the investment approach must be done very differently. One cannot invest a $100 million or more in the same way one invests ten million dollars.

A lot of families go into preservation mode because their appetite for risk was already waning. It is one thing to put at risk something when you don't know what its value is—it's a family business; it could be worth anything. When somebody pays money for it and actually assigns a dollar value to it, it suddenly *feels* so much more, and so their appetite for risk goes down even further. In other cases, they might try to continue to grow the family wealth, depending on the size of the family and the appetite of the family members to get involved.

What can easily happen next is that people become bored. In a business where family members are involved in it on some level, they have something to do on a day-to-day basis. But if the family is largely living from the income of passive assets and investments, then what do they do with their lives?

Another scenario after the first generation entrepreneur makes it is that they continue to grow the business and are able to successfully transition it to the second generation. In the second generation, there is usually more than one family member involved. Suddenly, the business that had one key stakeholder—the owner and founder—has multiple stakeholders. This leads to governance issues. How should the business be governed? Does the family want to diversify the business so that other family members can get involved without the risk of stepping on each other's toes? Sometimes that is successful, and sometimes the third generation puts the family assets at risk and loses them.

A lot of these paths end up with the third generation losing the money because they are putting it at risk. Why are they doing this? Often it is because they are bored and not as personally invested in the business as the previous generations or because there is conflict between the second and third generations that has been brewing and has until now stayed below the surface. Usually, it only comes to the surface after the previous generations are no longer around.

In the final scenario, the first generation creates wealth and manages to build a multi-generational diversified *empire,* which means the family wealth is no longer concentrated in a single business. Along the way, they may have acquired, or created, a number of businesses that are separate enough that the next generations can get involved without stepping on each other's toes. Being able to have a number of family members involved in the family businesses while maintaining their own autonomy is a good thing. On the other hand, you can end up with a situation of having too many cooks—too many family members—in charge of different parts of the empire. That can be a recipe for conflict or competitiveness within the family because their relative equity in the family wealth is no longer the same. Rather, they have different stakes in different divisions of a diversified set of assets, some of which may perform better than others. Some family members have the challenge of being in both ownership and management roles, while others are just passive owners.

That can lead to risk-taking, losing the money, or very often, the solution is a separation. When that happens, you don't quite start all over again, but the family assets are divided. Often the parts when separated are worth less than the whole—so the act of dividing the assets also results in the destruction of net equity. Many families end up doing this as a solution to the problem of how to manage the wealth together as a family. In the interest of peace and harmony, it can be better to separate out and let everybody go their own way and cut their own path rather than try and work together.

The second generation is so important because their job, as that *bridge* between the wealth originator and the grandchildren, is to transmit something meaningful to their children. They can only do that if they have something meaningful in their lives. That relies on the first generation transmitting something of substance to them.

In-Laws

The other thing you get with children are spouses, which in a family business context are a further complicating factor. Our children may choose to build their lives with a partner. That partner may come from a very different culture and bring their own financial circumstances. They also bring their own attitudes about wealth and their aspirations.

A person enters a family in one of two ways: birth or marriage. When you enter a family through birth, you are a family member for life. You may be estranged from your family, but the biological relationship can never be broken. Relationships that go up and down the generational tree, with your parents and with your children, can never be denied, and can never really go away. They are there. They may not be *good* relationships, but they are relationships nevertheless. Nobody ceases to be a parent and nobody ceases to be a child of somebody else. As the adage states: blood is thicker than water. Those blood relationships are very strong.

This contrasts with the other way to join a family: by marriage. In that case, you enter a family by marriage, and you exit a family by divorce (or death). Marriage is a wonderful thing (especially in the months leading up to the big day), and divorce is usually a very unpleasant thing. In my view, there is no such thing as an "amicable" divorce. I am fortunate to have been married for a long time, and during that time, many friends and acquaintances have divorced. It is rare that a divorced couple remains best buddies afterward.

Two clients of mine were married for over twenty-five years, but once the children were all grown up and moved out of the house, their marriage ended in a "gray divorce." The family business was held in a family trust, and one of their three children worked in it full time. The acrimonious nature of the divorce had serious implications: the wife wanted her fair share of the marital assets, and the children—two of whom were married with children themselves—were collateral damage as each parent sought to bring them on their side. The son who was in the business "sided" with his mother, which hurt his relationship with his father, whom he saw most days in a work context. Retaining ownership of the business with the possibility of a hostile major shareholder was impossible, and buying her out would create a huge debt burden, exacerbated by the difficult relationship between father and son.

They chose to sell the business for an amount which, while much less than its full worth, was still well above "fire sale" asset value. The father remained on for two years, but the son walked away, took a distribution, and bought a business for himself. Five years later, a number of family relationships remain in tatters.

Would a prenuptial agreement have helped here? Only to limit the payout to the wife, but not to prevent the relationship damage, and its separate effect on the family business.

Families that span multiple generations need to develop family policies to deal with these eventualities. A lot of families say that because this child relationship is unbreakable and the spouse relationship is, they don't want children-in-law involved in the family business in any way. They keep it to "blood only" for exactly that reason.

Since spouses come from a different family and bring a different culture, this too can be a potential source of conflict in a family. The child may be satisfied with something, but the spouse comes in and may have a number of motivations for marrying. One of them might be the attraction to wealth and the good life. They may have very different aspirations than what the family established for their children. This is yet another reason why, as we move into the second and third generation, things get very complicated. This is also a reason why some wealthy families prefer their children to marry into other wealthy families. To an extent, it takes that financial issue off the table. It is less likely that somebody is marrying for money if they too come from money. This is rather unfortunate, but it's a fact of life.

Family wealth can change over generations, the appetite for risk changes over generations, and things get more complicated, as I've explained. There are multiple stakeholders. When you are a wealth originator, you are the master of your own destiny. You have created the business. In many cases, you own all of the business and you can forge your own path. As soon as you have more stakeholders, they each have their own interests. They will have had more or less of a role in the continued growth of the family wealth and that also affects their position in regard to being custodians or managers of that wealth. The two key influences on how a family manages wealth when they are no longer the originators of that wealth are their relationships and their attitudes toward wealth.

Intergenerational Issues
Action Step

Go to your *Transition Workbook* and follow along with the Intergenerational Issues exercises. Take some time to identify your attitudes toward entrepreneurship and risk. Also, identify the attitudes of the generations before you and after you. To download your complimentary workbook, go to www.DavidWerdiger.com/transition-workbook

CHAPTER 6

Family Business: Burdens versus Opportunities

"In the middle of difficulty lies opportunity."
– Albert Einstein

Many people view family business and family wealth as a privilege. They think it is all roses. Why would anybody *not* want to be born into a family that has a family business where you do not have to go through the effort of starting from nothing? From the outside, it looks so picture perfect.

That is certainly one way to look at it. As they say, the grass is always greener on the other side. But there is also the notion that a family legacy is not just an opportunity, it is also a *burden.* We are all born into families, and those families have expectations of us. Being part of a family gives people an opportunity, but it also can weigh heavily when there are expectations of joining the family business, or performing some other role by virtue of your association with the family. Expectations can be a burden. They can weigh very heavily on you because you are not starting with your own "clean slate."

By way of an analogy, in the software world, when we develop a piece of software from scratch, we are starting from a clean slate. We can do whatever we want. We are not constrained by anything another developer has already done. However, when reworking or enhancing software that already exists, there are confines and limitations as to what can be done within the code. The same principle applies when considering changes to your house. If you pull it down and rebuild it, you are starting from a clean slate. On the other hand, if you want to renovate or remodel a home, then you have to work within the constraints of what already exists. That can lead to surprises and significantly higher costs than expected.

Legacy is simultaneously an opportunity and a burden. In the Jewish tradition, the Sages teach that "each of us must ask: 'When will my deeds reach those of my fathers—Abraham, Isaac and Jacob?'"[12] Everybody has to ask themselves, when will they live up to the deeds of their ancestors? That perfectly expresses the burden of legacy. It is based on the notion that our predecessors achieved more than us, and therefore, we have an obligation to achieve as much as them or greater. That can be a difficult thing to do, especially if you come from a family of high achievers.

Parents should consider their family business and determine what it is doing for them, what it is doing for their children, and what it can do (in the future) for their children. The children are looking at it from a different perspective. They might be saying, "I don't want to be in this family business. I appreciate it. What it does for me is it gives me a lifestyle, and that's a very good thing, and I must be grateful for that, but that doesn't mean that I need to be part of it and work in it. Previous generations have found

12 "The Height and Weight of Heroes—Torah.org." *The Height and Weight of Heroes—Torah.org.* Web.

personal fulfillment in working in the family business. I want to find fulfillment in some other way." They can find that fulfillment in whatever they want.

This is similar to the notion of individuation, of being your own person, as opposed to being the child of somebody else or a member of a certain family, which we discussed previously. Ultimately, everybody wants to be their own person.

Parents want what is best for their children, and what they often want for their children comes from a place of love. They see what they have done, and they want similar for their children. At the same time, parents don't often recognize that their children are very different. As we discussed, they don't recognize the different generational influences. They don't recognize the changes that have happened in the world during their lifetime, and that the values that they grew up with aren't the values that their children have grown up with. Children ought to be able to say that they want their own independence and to make their own choices in life. At the same time, they ought to be respectful of where the family wealth came from, and where those opportunities came from because they didn't come from nowhere. They happen to be born into a family that has wealth, and they ought to be grateful for it, not take it for granted. As the proverb says, "Don't look a gift horse in the mouth." It's a gift, and a sense of gratitude is appropriate.

That is balanced against the conflict between obligation, choice, and opportunity. Being born into a family with money comes with obligations to the family. At the very least, as mentioned, the obligation to be grateful, but it also comes with opportunities. The challenge is to balance those and understand what you really want, what other people in your family from your generation and from other generations want, and find something that meets as many different needs as possible.

These are the questions families have to ask themselves: What is the purpose of their business? Why does the family business exist? Does it exist to create wealth? Does it exist to give people something to do and to provide jobs for family members? More broadly, what is the purpose of any business enterprise for the owners? A family business is a business owned by a family. Why do they own it?

For a business whose life spans multiple generations, the answer is different depending on what generation you come from. For the people who founded the business—the wealth originators—the family business was a pathway to a particular place, and that might have been wealth. Once you already have that, how do you take that to the next generation and find meaning for the next generation?

Further to our earlier discussion about the relationship between a business and its owner, what is the relationship between the family and the family businesses or the family assets? Who is there to serve whom? It is to support the family's lifestyle or goals, or is being part of the family business the goal into itself? If so, what is the real goal?

The question becomes, what are your real goals? You want to create wealth, or to sustain wealth, or to grow wealth, but wealth isn't an end to itself. Each generation ought to ask themselves that simple question: what do you really want?

Do you want to have money? But what is money good for if not to spend and support a particular lifestyle? So perhaps what you want rather than money is a certain lifestyle. Which is more important: the money or the lifestyle? Can you have both? Some people want money to compete with others based on numbers or ranks in a list, and this is something that drives a lot of people. In that case, what they *really* want is to be better than others.

The first generation is often looking to get from a place where they are not financially secure to a place of financial security. That is only the case for the first generation.

The second generation, and subsequent generations who are already born into financial security, want something different. What they want is different because they are different people, and they are living in a different time, and they are their own individuals.

It is one thing for a wealth originator to say, "I am the head of this family, and I want this for my family." That's fine, but once the wealth originator moves on in whatever way, then the family has to ask itself, what do we want? There is a shift from an "I" to a "we," where "we" represents a diverse group of individuals with different interests. Asking what they want is a question many families fail to ask themselves.

I believe that the most important thing that family wealth gives a person is *choice:* they can do whatever they want. Warren Buffett once said, "I want to give my kids just enough so that they would feel that they could do anything, but not so much that they would feel like doing nothing."[13] That represents this notion that you can do anything if you have money, but you could also do nothing. Doing anything represents the promise of opportunity and choice. Doing nothing is, by definition, an empty life.

Somebody who does not work, who doesn't do anything, who just lives off the family assets, is exhibiting a parasitic behavior where all one does is take and take. Choice is good, but equally, one can choose to do nothing. That too is a choice, just not a good one.

Work ethic matters; people need to be productive. I'll draw on

13 Willett, Megan. "15 Tycoons Who Won't Leave Their Fortunes To Their Kids." Business Insider. Business Insider, 20 Aug. 2013. Web.

my religion where it says in the Bible, "Man was born to toil" (Job 5:7). The extreme attitude toward wealth where parents spoil their children and give them everything they want is not productive; children cannot develop a work ethic with such an upbringing. People were put on this earth to do something.

It is possible to have a work ethic even though you don't need to work and all of your material needs are satisfied. Having a work ethic means you can do something productive. It doesn't have to be for earning money, but it can be for helping other people. There is no shortage of productive things you can do if you have a work ethic.

Subsequent generations who are born into wealth have these choices, but it comes out to the old adage, "With great power comes great responsibility." You have choices to do things, but you can make good choices or bad choices.

People who do not have those choices are sometimes in a better position because they need to work. They need to be productive in order to reach a level of financial security they are comfortable with. Somebody who is the child, or the grandchild, of an entrepreneur is not driven by finances. They have too many choices. They are spoilt for choice, and they do not need to work.

Parents often say, "I worked in this business. I want my children to work in this business." That is a nice sentiment. However, that is what you want, but what do your children want? When my children were little, I said, "What do you want to do when you grow up?" My sons said, "I want to go in Daddy's business." Why? Because they saw this notion of continuity. They are continuing something that their father started, and they're continuing that family dynasty and legacy. That was nice to hear from my children because it indicated they admired me and, therefore, want to be like me (as a contrast, consider the song "Cat's in the Cradle"). It is flattering for a parent to see their children continuing what they do. It means that their children valued what they do enough that they want to do it, too.

After further reflection, and study, and looking at family businesses, I thought: *why* do I want my children to do that? They don't have to do that just because I did it. They are different people. What I want to give my children, and I think the greatest gift that any parent can give their children, are the *choices* to be their own person and the *options* to do whatever they want. That still has to be tempered by the notion of encouraging them to choose to do positive things with their lives, while still giving them those choices. Don't make them feel obliged to be part of the family business. If they feel obliged to be part of the family business, then they are serving the family business instead of the family business serving them. There is a double-edged sword of obligation and opportunity.

Bringing Children into the Business

If the children decide they do want to be part of the business, but they also want to forge their own paths within the construct of the family business, the parents must first recognize that it is the children's choice. Then comes the hard part—the mechanics of it determining a place for each child in the family business. What should their jobs be?

Are they able to get on with other family members who are also in the family business? If the family business is big enough, hopefully, they can find a place where each child, or each family member who chooses to get involved, can be involved and be their own person.

When you are bringing family members into a family business, it is important for them to earn their position. Any business ought to be a meritocracy. If family members are being given preferential treatment because of who they are, this conflicts with the principle of meritocracy. That is nepotism.

The challenge of bringing a family member into a family business is that other people, whether family members or other employees in the business, look at this person and say, "I earned my place here. What about you?" What the directors or board members need to do is create a position for each child, for each person, to come into the business. They need to do so in a way that recognizes the fact that they've earned their position in part by birth. They need to make sure that the children genuinely earn their position, and that they genuinely make a contribution that, by objective standards, is rewarded appropriately. It is imperative that they are paid for their work in alignment with their replacement cost. This brings us to the principles behind operating a family business as a meritocracy, which is very difficult.

One part of this is making sure people entering the family business do not come in raw. They have to get a bit of external experience in the outside world that they can draw from. First of all, to make sure that they are suitably qualified for the positions they are taking. Second of all, they can bring a new perspective into the family and make a contribution to the family business by providing a new way of looking at things.

Family Business Burdens versus Opportunities Action Step

Go to your *Transition Workbook* and follow along with the Family Business Burdens versus Opportunities exercises. Take some time to identify your burdens and opportunities. Additionally, identify your goals and connection to the family business. To download your complimentary workbook, go to www.DavidWerdiger.com/transition-workbook

CHAPTER 7

Developing Trust in Your Business

"A business fails when motive becomes more important than trust."
– Thiruman Archunan

In any business, it is important that trust is developed. In a multi-generational family business, where there is an overlay of multi-faceted relationships, establishing trust among all members of the group is especially essential. This chapter explores some of the effective strategies used to create a safe environment within a business.

Establishing Rules

Many family businesses have rules in place regarding operations and finances. It is good for families to have rules, but it's equally important for families to understand *why* the rules are in place, whether or not the rules are serving the family interests, and whether or not, at some point, the rules need to change because the family interests or attitudes have changed. This chapter begins with some examples of rules families impose on the way they operate and the way they manage the family wealth.

Types of Rules

One multi-generational family I have worked with diversified into a few different businesses, and a fair number of family members (about fifteen) work in the family businesses. They have a rule that at family gatherings, nobody is allowed to talk business. At times, a rule like that can be very difficult to abide by, but it's a rule that works in the interests of the family.

This rule is essentially about managing the boundaries between personal life and the family assets. If life *is* the family assets, and if every time the family gets together, they talk business, they are slaves to their businesses, and a slave to their assets, rather than their assets delivering value to their lives.

I've seen another family business where two family members always end up talking business whenever they meet socially. Why is this such a bad thing? Firstly, it's a distraction from the social occasion. Secondly, it means they aren't taking a break from business life. Thirdly, their personal relationship (as first cousins) is almost non-existent. Fourthly, the setting doesn't allow for what could become a very vigorous and robust discussion. If there is a strong difference of opinion on a business matter, are they really going to be able to deal with it adequately at his mother's house for Sunday brunch? Consider the risks to their personal relationship if a business matter came between them. There are many reasons why mixing personal and business matters is unhealthy, both for them as individuals and for the family business itself.

There are also rules about who is allowed and who isn't allowed to work in the family business. These rules are about *trust.* In a previous chapter, we identified some of the challenges that marriage brings to a family business. These rules are about recognizing that a person comes into a family through birth or marriage, and leaves a family through death or divorce. People have no choice regarding birth and death, but people do have a choice regarding marriage and divorce; therefore, when somebody who is involved in the family business may at some time in the future leave that family, there is the potential for future conflict. That is the basis for the rule that some families have—that only blood family members are involved in managing the family assets, because blood family members are family members until the day they die, as opposed to people who marry in.

There are also rules about what one has to do in order to be allowed to join the family business or to join that group that manages the family assets. These are about making sure the family business is run as a meritocracy. These types of rules are extremely important because nepotism—favoring people simply because they happen to be relatives—is bad in any business or organization. It leads to conflict of interest, jealousy, and poor decision making, and it can limit the potential of employees.

Achieving Role Separation

Rules such as these can help achieve a separation between the family and its assets, between ownership, stewardship, governance, management, and employment. Those are all terms that describe the roles a person or group of people have with respect to a financial asset.

The key separation should be between ownership and management. There can be many owners of a business, but there are limits to how many people can manage or work in a business. Public companies can have many thousands, or even millions, of shareholders, but only a small number of people are ultimately responsible as directors of the company, as board members, or as managers. In classic management theory, the agency model prescribes that these people are acting on behalf of the owners, but are separate from the owners. Families able to implement such a structure effectively reduce conflict as much as possible.

Family Business Culture of Acceptance

In my business, we have a rule whenever somebody new starts in the company. We instruct them to question everything. The rule in the business is that it's not acceptable to say, "We do this because this is the way we've always done it." For my business, this rule enables fresh views to improve existing processes. Simply allowing such questions to be asked is a huge step.

When a family member joins the family business, they are coming into the business essentially because they are a family member. Others might infer that this is the way we do things around here—that we reward people because of who they are and who their parents are. If you want to run a family business as a meritocracy, that sends the wrong message.

A better approach is to say to the family member: "You have been given the opportunity to join the family business because of who you are, but it stops there. That is the limit to the privilege that you've been assigned purely as a result of birth. You still need to have the requisite preparation, which might mean getting a job externally, finding yourself externally, before coming into the family business and making a contribution there."

Imagine a situation where someone in a business has been there for many years and manages the financials by hand on paper. Then someone from a younger generation joins and says, "We should move this onto a computer or online system. That makes more sense. It's going to make it easier. It's going to save us money. We are going to be able to look at other aspects of how the business works as opposed to just what's written out here on the paper, and we can get some better numbers and track everything better."

You might think that in the twenty-first century, this is an absurd example, but it has happened far more often than we might expect.

The instinctive response of the older generation employee might be to put their foot down and exert their seniority and authority: "We are sticking with paper. This is the way we've always done these things." However, that's not a good position to take.

The approach to this conflict requires latitude on the parts of both generations. The older generation has to allow space for the next generation to come in, and have input, and suggest better ways of doing things. The younger generation has to have a modicum (or more) of respect for what they are coming into, and not just be disruptive and say it has to be done this new way because this is the way the world is doing things now.

Avoiding conflicts like this comes down to the owners of the family business establishing an environment and a culture where suggesting these things is acceptable. That is where it starts. It starts with the family, and/or the family board, saying the culture of this family business is that we welcome new ways of doing things.

The family business culture needs to be set by the family leadership and/or the family board. It starts with creating the space where it is acceptable to have these sorts of dialogues, where we can say that just because somebody from the next generation comes in, we don't reject what they say simply because of who they are, but rather we accept and have a dialogue about whether this is the best way to do things. Are there other ways we should be looking at things or other ways of doing things that could be beneficial to our business?

The starting point to even begin those discussions and not immediately have the opinions of the next generations stomped on, simply because they are less senior members of the family, is with the family leadership making a clear statement. In embodying the culture of the family business, you have to explicitly declare that it is the culture of this family business that we accept suggestions from younger members of the family, and we respect the older generation. We also have a dialogue between generations. Ask if is there a better way to do things or if you should be doing something differently.

This is just another example of the business being a meritocracy—where decisions are made on their merit rather than looking at the people behind those decisions (or suggestions).

As previously mentioned, the family business culture is a reflection of the family culture, just like a person's business culture is a reflection of their personal values. It actually begins with the family culture itself welcoming the next generation and the views of the next generation. You have to be open to having that dialogue. You can't say, "In the business, we operate one way, but in the wider family, we operate another way." You need to have that *congruence of values* between the way the family works in general, and the way the family business works. Those are the foundations for being able to have these discussions and have them not falling very quickly into conflict.

If you can't get on as a family, you have no hope of getting on as a business. The family business values have to flow from the family values. If you can't get along personally, you can't only fix it in the context of the family business. You have to fix it in the context of the family in general.

Reducing Power Struggles

Power struggles often arise in families, as distinct from corporations, because people have dual roles (that doesn't mean they don't arise in corporations, rather they happen for different reasons). In a family, someone might be an owner, or part-owner, but also work in the family business. How does one determine the compensation for such a person? Ownership, or equity, is something a person might inherit, and is by nature passive: once you get it, it's yours. On the other hand, managing the family business means being there regularly, and working on behalf of everybody else. You may receive a salary as a manager, but because you are also going in there with the owner role, you might put in more than you would otherwise. The owner invariably puts in more effort, and the owner-manager loses sleep the way no employee does because their exposure to the business is far greater, and they can't just walk away the way an employee can.

An employee has a job, and a job has requirements on them, and it pays a salary. If the employee is not happy, they can leave and, hopefully, find another job. When you own a business, or when you are a part owner of a family business, you worry about it. Multiple hats in a family business, especially when there are more and more family members and more generations, can create power struggles. People can't necessarily maintain a clear boundary between their role working for the business, and their status as an owner of a business.

What it all comes down to is determining a way to recognize the role of a family member working in the business, as opposed to another family member who doesn't. The way to do it effectively is with separation of powers, such as having a family council that is responsible for the assets and management, and where they act on behalf of all the other owners. As hard as it is to make families work more like corporations with respect to their assets, it is beneficial. Even then, there may still be power struggles, because some people in the family might believe they are better than others or feel entitled to a position in the business.

There are many reasons why family businesses can have power struggles, and they are not always avoidable. The first step is to understand why they occur. Often, it is because of conflicts of interest, because different family members have different relationships with the family assets. It is quite possible that they occur less when family members are not involved in the family business, where the assets are all passive, and managed by somebody else. There is less to argue about. It is easier to make an external manager accountable than it is to make your sister accountable. But equally, they may occur as proxies for the sorts of rivalries and struggles that exist in any family.

Mark was a loving husband, father, and grandfather who built up a prosperous business which supported his and his three children's families. Two of the children were actively involved, but the father retained control and made all major decisions. When he became ill in his early eighties and had to reduce his hours due to treatment, things continued as usual without any major handover to the children. The business was mature and stable enough to run without him being there full time. However, when a further setback led to his rapid decline and death, suddenly the children had to deal with his lack of good estate planning. The children were uncomfortable with the level of debt, so they sold off some assets. With the father no longer around as a dominant presence in the family, some of the latent relationship issues between the children came to the surface, and this had a negative impact on the business. The siblings in the business established a board with an independent chairman to help them move forward, and are still working together.

Financial Risks

Trust needs to be developed around the business's finances. A family business deals with a different set of challenges than a corporation does when it comes to making investment decisions. The following table highlights some of the major differences between a Professional Investor and a Family Office. The unique emotional challenges and unknown factors make trust-building essential when making financial decisions as a family.

Corporation vs Family

	Professional Investor	Family (Office)
Accountable to	Shareholders, board	Family members, family board?
Risk Profile	Usually well understood	??
Culture	Usually known	Can be diverse, lots of 'legacy'
How they deal with failure	Move on, usually not much emotion	Cold silence across the dinner table?
How to join	Get a job	Birth & marriage
How to leave	Resign and move on	Enter a world of pain ☹

As mentioned, one of the key differences between a family and a corporation is how one joins or leaves. This also has implications for the family investment decision process. There is not an emotional attachment to a corporation the same way there is to a family. Your relationship with a family, as opposed to a corporation, is a deeper relationship that lasts much longer. It is a relationship that is more difficult, sometimes impossible, to exit.

Now, think about the elements of investment decisions that apply to corporations as opposed to a family. In a corporation, the management is accountable to the shareholders, through the governance of the board. That is a typical accountability structure for a corporation. In the case of a family or family office, these structures depend on the unique aspects of the family. As they say, "If you've seen one family, you've seen one family." Every family is different; every family has different ways they account to themselves, and that is a function of several things, such as where the wealth sits generationally, and whether the wealth originator is still around. If they are, then generally they're very much in control and accountable to nobody, which is their right as the wealth originator. However, as the family moves to subsequent generations, this can change significantly. That transition is a very bumpy one and is often not at all like the accountability that exists within a corporation.

The other area of difference is risk profile. A corporation generally has a greater awareness of its risk profile than a family business; a family doesn't always articulate theirs. This function of governance also arises because a family's wealth concentration can take significant shifts, especially as the family evolves from one generation to another. The culture of a corporation is set by the leadership of the company and is usually fairly well articulated.

Alternatively, the culture of a family is diverse, it changes, and it has influences with each successive generation, in particular, by marriage as new people of possibly diverse cultures join the family.

The biggest difference between the way a corporation invests and the way a family invests is how they deal with failure. A corporation may make an investment decision that turns out to be bad, but when that happens, they usually move on and do the next thing. On the other hand, particularly in a family that invests *in* family members, it can end up with very awkward situations. The classic example is across the dinner table or at Christmas dinner where everybody is getting together and shooting nasty looks at the family member who lost a lot of the family money, or had a fantastic idea, asked for some money from the family to fund it, and then blew it.

With corporate investment, the leadership is very clearly top down, and the corporation has a respected hierarchy. With families, that is not always the case. This is where families can get stuck in investing. The younger members of the family or future generations, younger generations, want to make their own decisions and have their own autonomy. In the corporate world, there is a clear hierarchy; in a family, there isn't a clear hierarchy. This is a feature of how families work, and families have to deal with the different hierarchical structure and the different cultures and attitudes that are floating around within the same family.

Relationship Risk

The other thing to consider in family investment decisions is the additional dimension of risk. Corporations are in the business of managing risk. Families, particularly family offices that have assets being managed by the family or invested by family members, have an entirely new dimension to their risk—*relationship risk.* A family member might go into a relationship with another family member and make a lot of money, but in the process, they end up with a very dysfunctional personal relationship because they are relatives. Again, going back to an important theme that was introduced earlier, there is not a clear barrier between the family investment self and the family member self. In a family business or office, the roles become blurred. That is where relationship risk can have an adverse effect on how the family business does things.

To reduce the risk, the first thing members of the business need to do is recognize this thing called relationship risk—the key to managing any risk is to understand that the risk exists. Then start to think about how to manage it. The way to manage any risk is usually diversification; don't put all your eggs in one basket when investing. Similarly, you shouldn't put all your eggs in one basket in terms of family members. Treat family members and the investments that are being run by family members as a diversified set of investments.

The goal is, as stated, to separate these things as much as possible, to the extent that it is possible, which means having strong family governance so that the family is actively managing the relationship risks. That relationship risk should be a part of every investment decision as a different aspect of risks that the business takes.

Form Alliances

Another way to mitigate this risk is to form alliances with other families. One strength of families is that they are tight-knit and they have access to capital. But on the other hand, it can be very difficult for family members to work together and maintain boundaries. It is also very difficult for family members to mentor other family members because there is emotional baggage between them. Mentoring is very important and beneficial for the recipient. However, the best mentor is *not* always a family member. Often, relatives don't know how to keep the right emotional distance between the mentor and the mentee because they are bringing too much else to the table. To deal with this, create alliances with other families who understand the family dynamic and who understand how families work. Two family businesses can work together, where the older generation of one family mentors the younger generation of the other family. That allows each to tap into that family experience and get the benefits of that, but still be able to maintain just the right amount of emotional distance to have a functional intergenerational mentor relationship. It is really powerful when families can help other families.

Have Open Discussions

Finally, families need to be able to have open discussions. Every family will have a culture and a way they do things, and there will be disruptions to that culture, so the most important thing families have to learn how to do is be able to discuss those changes and not allow them to remain the elephant in the room. They can't just slam the door on any new way of doing things that a family member comes up with. A family member may come up with ideas from external influence or just because they are a part of a new generation, and they look at the world differently.

As more generations join the business, each member needs to feel that they are a member of a business with a culture of acceptance. Clear rules and roles are in place, and everyone is comfortable contributing to discussions and the future of the business.

Developing Trust in Your Business Action Step

Go to your *Transition Workbook* and follow along with the Developing Trust in Your Business exercises. Take some time to identify relationship risks in your family business. Identify the rules established in your business.

To download your complimentary workbook, go to www.DavidWerdiger.com/transition-workbook

CHAPTER 8

Intergenerational Wealth Transfer

"True wealth is not measured in money or status or power. It is measured in the legacy we leave behind for those we love and those we inspire."

– Cesar Chavez

There is a huge amount of wealth that has been accumulated—created by the foundation generation and Baby Boomers—that is in the process of being transitioned to the next generation. It is the greatest intergenerational wealth transfer that has ever occurred in history.

According to one *MarketWatch* article, "the richest Americans are preparing to transfer *$6 trillion* in assets over the next three decades."[14] While much of this transfer of wealth is occurring in the US, this is happening all over the world. In many cases, this transfer is happening during the lifetime of the wealth originators, or the people who added significantly to the wealth. This transfer poses many challenges to both the people who are on the giving side and on the receiving side of the wealth. How can one transmit something that is meaningful, and that is more than just money?

[14] Fottrell, Quentin. "Prepare for the Largest Wealth Transfer in History." *MarketWatch*. 31 Jan. 2015. Web.

Make the Business an Asset

If I have a business, how do I transition that into something of value to my children, or to the next generation? There are various strategies we are going to cover, but the first step to doing that is making the business an asset itself. You can only transmit an asset if it is indeed an asset. If your business is worthless (or worth a lot less) without *you* in it, then what are you actually transmitting? This goes back to the difference between owning a job and owning a company. What makes a company an asset is its intrinsic value independent of the owners. The key to transmitting any asset is to make sure that it has intrinsic value without the owners being involved.

Imagine a family business where the owner is a key person, and the business revolves around them as an individual. If the owner decides to bring his son into the business, then from the perspective of everyone else (customers, suppliers, staff), little has changed. The business still revolves around the owner, and the son will be viewed as the owner's son, rather than the owner. It takes a lot for the son to be viewed as the owner, particularly because customers of the business identify the business with the owner, not with the son of the owner. The key step of being able to transfer a business to the next generation is making sure that the business has intrinsic value on its own—that it's not too tied to the owner and the owner's personality. That way, the owner actually has something to transmit.

As discussed earlier, I define *owning a job* as being self-employed full time in a role that is essential to your business. This is a small yet important step up from having a job because you are working for yourself. At the same time, if you own a *job,* transitioning that to somebody else is very hard because the job is you, and you are the job, and they are almost inseparable. Getting somebody else to take your place and to take over ownership of that job is very difficult. On the other hand, if you own the *business,* your relationship with the business is as the owner, and the business is over there. The owner and the business are separate things, and the business is there to serve the owner.

In order to successfully transition a business from one generation to the next, the business needs to be a separate entity from the owner. That way, a new owner, or a group of owners, can come in and take over the owner role, and the business can continue to do what it does under a new stewardship. The nature of the owner's relationship is, therefore, of owning a business, not owning a job.

Scott ran the family business with an iron fist. His was the first and last word on anything. He didn't have the time or the appetite for such things as family board, committees, and the many advisors his children suggested they get involved to help with succession planning. He had seen way too many of his contemporaries go down this path, even to the point of divesting their wealth to their children during their lifetimes, only to see their children squander them. He knew what was best for them, and he could generate superior returns. It made perfect sense to remain in charge for as long as he possibly could. He remained sprightly and energetic even into his early eighties.

But the stroke was brutal and left him bedridden, partially paralyzed, and while he retained his mental faculties, speech was slow and difficult. His wife and children faced a difficult decision—the business was so dependent on him, but the children were in their fifties and had little desire to turn their lives around and suddenly get involved in the family business. They appointed a large accounting firm to manage the company with a view to a complete exit within twelve months. The financial outcome was good, but this spelled the end of the family business, as all the children went their own ways.

Change Your Emotional Relationship

If you feel that you own a job rather than a business, that doesn't mean you are not able to make a change. You may be at a stage either in your life, or in the life of the business, when you will need others to play a more important role in the business. As discussed, the first step is to change your *emotional relationship* with the business. You have to recognize what the business is for. Is it here to provide you a job—with something to do every day—or is it here to serve you or support your lifestyle? The key shift is from thinking that the business is what you do when you get up in the morning to the business as something that is there to support you, to support your lifestyle, and to meet your needs.

Identify Your Roles

Once you make that psychological and emotional shift, then the next step is to identify your roles in the business. What are the roles that you are occupying in this business? Business founders and owners who are deeply invested in their business usually occupy multiple roles. What often comes with being a founder is the view that nobody else can perform those roles better than they can.

Once you identify the roles you perform in your business, it's OK to acknowledge that you might be the best person to perform those roles, but at the same time, you can't do everything. Somebody who grows a business from scratch goes through a process like this because when a person starts a business, they start off doing everything, and as it grows, they slowly divest themselves of roles. This is the process described in Michael Gerber's book *The E-myth,* and it is a process that I followed with several of my businesses. The hardest part was fighting against the belief that I couldn't let someone else take over a role because I was much better than them in that role.

The key is to step back and acknowledge that while you can do those better than anyone, you cannot do *all* of the roles. Your time is limited. The question then becomes: how to resolve the conflict between having the roles completed in the best possible way, and having all of the roles completed? The answer is that it meets your needs as owner for other people to do these same roles, even though they are not doing it as well as you can. Accept that other people can fulfill roles—maybe not as well as you; however, it's in the best interest of the business to have other people fulfilling those roles.

This stems from the principle that the business here is to serve your lifestyle. If you want to go away for a month and have other people taking on various responsibilities, then it is in the interest of the business to have other people performing these roles.

Using this methodology, you can head down a path of divesting yourself of some of the day-to-day roles of the business, and shifting, as Michael Gerber said, "From working *in* the business to working *on* the business." When you start to make that shift, you are shifting from owning a job to owning a business. You are able to step back from the business, look at it and recognize that it is something separate from yourself—something that has a life of its own. This is a move toward working *on* the business—governing (in addition to managing) the business.

Once you are governing the business and still have some operational roles in the business, it becomes clear when you are sitting in a governance role, and when you are sitting in an operations role. I was able to do this in my business when I had multiple roles, even to the point where I had employed a CEO. The CEO's role is to run the business on a day-to-day basis, and following that important shift, I maintained two roles in the business. One is as the owner (and chair of the advisory board) where my job is to appoint the CEO, and the CEO works for me, and I set the strategic direction. That is my role in the business as the owner.

My parallel role in that business was an interesting one. I said to the CEO, "I started this business, and therefore, there are a lot of things I can do to help. If you want me to come and do those things, I'm here to do that." In that case, I'm actually working *for* the CEO, because the CEO was fully empowered to run the business on behalf of the owners. If the CEO identifies a resource that the business needs, for example, for the business owner to attend pre-sales meetings or to use his network, then in that case, the business owner is actually working in the business, but working for the CEO. Initially, I changed my title from Managing Director to Chairman. More recently, it changed to Chief Evangelist.

This is something I was able to do very effectively in my business because I was able to understand the separation of these roles as the owner. As the owner, I am responsible for governance and strategic direction, but at the same time, I'm doing what the business needs from me as a resource. My ego isn't so big that such tasks are beneath me—rather, it means I can do what the business needs at any given time, and I don't have to work 24/7 like I used to. I'm still able to make a contribution in a different modality, in a different way of working where sometimes I choose to work for the CEO and to do the things that the CEO needs because the CEO is running the business.

If you want your business to be an asset that you can pass on, then you need to take the time to go through these psychological and operational steps. It's freeing, and it can shift many aspects of your life for the better; you just have to make it happen.

Intergenerational Wealth Transfer Action Step

Go to your *Transition Workbook* and follow along with the Intergenerational Wealth Transfer exercises. In this section, identify the financial changes that have occurred in your life, your attitude toward wealth, and the lessons you want to pass to the next generation about wealth. To download your complimentary workbook, go to www.DavidWerdiger.com/transition-workbook

CHAPTER 9

How Much Is Enough?

"We make a living by what we get,
but we make a life by what we give."
– Winston Churchill

How much is enough? Remember, money can't buy happiness. Many people dream of so-called "f*** you" money. This fantasy is about having more than enough—enough that you don't have to work, enough that you can say to the people that you previously might have relied on financially, "F*** you!" While it may be fun to think about, that amount of money is far more than what you'll ever need. This chapter is not about the fantasy; rather, it is about taking a realistic look at how much you need to take care of yourself and future generations.

Begin by looking at your own family. For most people, that means making sure that the kids are looked after in the short- and long-term. What might you do for your kids? Given your values and lifestyle, what does it mean in practical terms to you to look after family? Do you focus on just your children, or do you also want to take care of other family members and future generations?

As an example, I did this exercise with my own family. After the tragic losses of the Second World War, my parents wanted to rebuild, and they did. In the second generation, there are five of us, plus spouses. The third generation has twenty-eight grandchildren, plus twenty-three spouses. The fourth generation—the great-grandchildren—is seventy and counting! We are a very large family by most standards. The *fertility rate* in our family (average number of children born to a woman during her lifetime) is around 4.5, and our family's growth rate (including spouses) since the mid-1970s is nearly 7%.

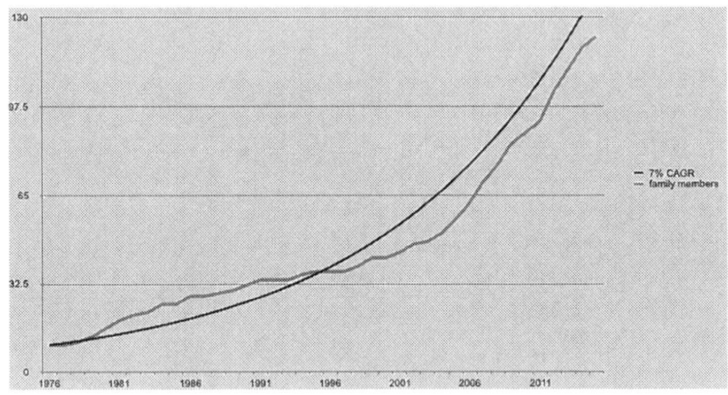

Growth rate of my non-average family

For wealth planning purposes, our family is *not* a very relevant example. Average fertility rates in the Western world hover around 2.0, which is barely replacement. However, wealthy families tend to have more children.[15][16] So for this exercise, let's consider a fertility rate of 3.0. The conversion of this rate into a population growth rate

15 Julie Zeveloff May 26, 2015, 7:00 AM. "The Ultimate Status Symbol among the Millionaire Mums of the Upper East Side Is Not What You'd Expect." *Business Insider Australia*. 25 May 2015. Web.

16 Doward, Jamie. "High-fliers Have More Babies, According to Study." *The Observer*. Guardian News and Media, 25 Oct. 2014. Web.

within a family is a complex one and depends on the mix of ages across multiple generations. For the purpose of this example, let's say it's 4%. This figure is very important, as we will see.

The next step is to map out, in broad terms, how the family will continue to support family members in the medium- to long-term. For example, let's say the family wants to do the following:

- Education: pay for a college education for each family member—let's call it $100K when they turn eighteen
- Housing: help them purchase a home—say $1M when they turn twenty-five
- Lifestyle: extra distributions annually to each adult child to supplement their lifestyle—say, $50K per child over twenty-one per year
- Take everyone on a vacation together once a year—say $200K

I have pulled these numbers out of a hat—they vary wildly depending on where you live, and your living standards. That establishes how the family aspires to deploy its wealth for the benefit of the family.

The next step is to consider some financial scenarios and calculate how much it will take to cover these expenses for each of your children, their children, and their children. Given those numbers, how much money will you actually need? With the help of an actuary (the career recommendation I rejected), this can easily be calculated and projected for fifty years—about two generations. This will determine how much you need to have in assets based on inflation, taking into account the likely return on the assets. It answers the simple question: how much capital do you need in order to provide this for your family?

Required Capital		Scenario
Inflation of 2.5%	No Inflation	
$53M	$31M	4% annual return
$19M	$12M	8% annual return

The effect of inflation is very important. $100K might buy a good college education now, but in a generation, it will cost more than double that. In order to stay ahead of the game, *the net returns on the family assets must outstrip both inflation and the organic growth of the family itself.* Bear in mind that dividends paid to family members are not reinvested.

Calculations like this are a useful reference point. Every family is different in so many ways: size, growth, aspirations, nature of their assets. It can be argued that families need to do more than just *preserve* their wealth; rather, they need to *grow* their wealth, which means they might be attracted to other asset classes, such as entrepreneurial risk.

This is also a great exercise in setting boundaries. When families grow, they grow exponentially, in the true meaning of the word. Sometimes, you might think you have great wealth, but when you add it all up, maybe the amount of money you have is not going to last as long as you thought when you extend the calculation beyond just one generation. It does put some real numbers on the table, in a tangible way, but also, it gets you thinking forward, thinking into the future and really doing some long-term planning with your family's wealth.

Now, it could be that you do this calculation, and in the case of your family, there will still be so much wealth remaining that it seems meaningless. In that case, if that gap is very large, then it's worth considering what the wealth is for. What are you going to do with it? Is it going to sit there and be conservatively managed or preserved in perpetuity? If it's not doing anything for your family, if you have more than enough for the next three generations, and there's still plenty, what is that money doing? What purpose is it serving? Do you need to have it?

This could give rise to family discussions about philanthropy. At the high end of the wealth spectrum, The Giving Pledge is a commitment by the world's wealthiest individuals and families to dedicate the majority of their wealth to philanthropy.[17] It's recognition that they do indeed have way more than "enough," and can, therefore, apply that wealth for a greater good.

Mary grew up in the Bible Belt and was taught from a young age the importance of tithing. Her business started there, but it expanded and moved to California. She was meticulous and exact in her accounting, and every year would distribute one tenth of profits into a foundation so it was clearly sequestered for charitable purposes. As her children grew up, she started to involve them in discussions about where to give the charity. After her sixty-fifth birthday, she shifted ten percent of ownership of her company to a foundation, so she could perpetuate her giving.

She took a similarly rigorous approach to looking after the long-term needs of her family. She engaged an actuary to calculate the cost to ensure subsequent generations received generous distributions for their education and housing. A share of the company was also transferred into a trust, separately managed, which would be responsible for these distributions as each family

17 "The Giving Pledge :: Pledger Profiles." The Giving Pledge :: Pledger Profiles. Web.

member came of age. The education component was "use it or lose it": if a family member declined to embark on some form of post-school education, they were unable to cash it in for something else. The family members remained actively involved in the foundation.

For any family, there is a number that is *enough*. Then, there's the gap between enough and what you have. Put some very rough numbers together, while recognizing that there is a gap and that there is such a thing as enough. When you have done that, you have created a plan for the future of your family's wealth while knowing that there is a target number that will provide for your family for generations to come.

How Much Is Enough?
Action Step

Go to your *Transition Workbook* and follow along with the How Much Is Enough? exercises. Take some time to identify what you want to do with your money and what you want to provide for your children.
To download your complimentary workbook, go to www.DavidWerdiger.com/transition-workbook

CHAPTER 10

Raising Children with Wealth

"Don't educate your children to be rich. Educate them to be happy, so they know the value of things, not the price."
– Brian Tracy

Raising children with wealth is not easy. The key is to find that middle ground where you don't spoil your children, you don't lavish them with every comfort there is, but you nevertheless provide them a good life. It's important to teach children that a dollar is still worth something. To do that, you need to value a dollar yourself; do not throw away money because, relative to your wealth, it is worth effectively zero. Even a dollar has value, so it's important to teach children, particularly as they're growing up, to value money.

A friend of mine—a psychologist—was counseling a married couple that sought his help resolving a huge fight over what car to buy their sixteen-year-old child. One partner wanted to buy him a brand new Bentley convertible, and the other one said, "No, no, no. Don't be silly. A second-hand one will be just fine." This is an extreme but true example of people who aren't living in the real world. You might believe that because you have wealth, you don't need to live in the same world as most others (the 99%), and to some extent, this is true. Depending on their level of wealth, people can live a very different life that can seem other-worldly. The question is, what sort of world do they want their children to grow up in, and what sort of values do they want them to have, particularly with respect to wealth, and respect to having meaning in life?

This is where that generational difference between people who grew up through a significant change in their financial situation and those who didn't comes into play. That could mean going from very financially tight to being comfortable, or from being at a certain level of financial comfort to a significantly higher level. People who have experienced a significant shift in their financial status upward, as opposed to people who were born after that shift, have very different attitudes toward money because they remember a time when their wealth wasn't there. In the example above, the older generation might remember a time when they couldn't get the Bentley convertible, but the younger generation doesn't know any different. They are the lesser for it because they don't have the opportunity to learn the value of a dollar. This is essentially the challenge of raising children with wealth: to teach them the value of a dollar, *despite the fact that they don't need to.*

To a large extent, this is about "tough love." You need to teach them that even though you *can* afford something, it is in the children's best interest that you do not just give it to them, so they can learn how to earn it. There is more to life than having money, and the purpose of money (and indeed life), is not purely to spend and consume. What life do you want your children to have? Do you want them to live a life of meaningless luxury, or do I want them to balance that with having some purpose in their life?

Meaning Beyond Money

It is important to explicitly teach children what wealth is, and how to have a meaningful life, even with wealth. It is a very big challenge to find meaning if you don't have to work a day in your life. A family may have sufficient wealth for several generations. If you don't have to work a day in your life, ever, then what do you actually *do* with your life? How do you find meaning in your life, and how do you avoid descending into hedonism and antisocial behavior, just because you can? That is the challenge of great wealth. As a wise friend once told me, "The poor want to be rich, and the rich want to be happy."

As the following graph shows, as growth increases, it impacts one's appetite for risk, value of a dollar, and overall happiness. Contrary to what many might assume, after a certain point, the increase in wealth decreases the other three factors. However, it is possible to find meaning and happiness in life, even with incredible wealth.

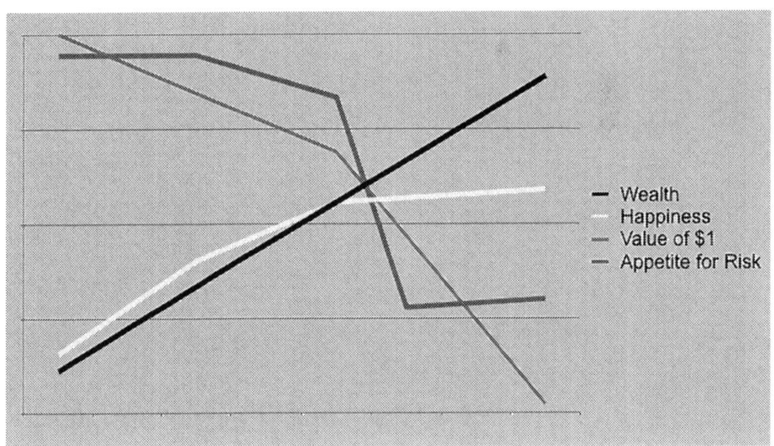

How do you do it? By keeping yourself grounded in the regular world. You have to retain some of your own original values about the value of a dollar. The more wealth you have, the less the marginal value of a dollar. But for many others, a dollar is still worth a dollar. A single dollar might not add anything to your life, but there are other people for whose lives it would make a difference, whether it's a dollar or a thousand dollars.

Decide how to have a meaningful life when money is not important, and money is not a limit on anything you do. If you don't need to work, what are you going to do with your life? If you're not working to increase your net wealth, then why do you get up in the morning? That's the question that you have to ask yourself.

Avoid Extremes

The key to finding the middle ground is to identify and then avoid lifestyle *extremes.* There are people who have great wealth yet live like paupers without spending their wealth or enjoying any of the finer things—living their lives as if they were indeed poor. Even though they have a lot of money tucked away in some assets, they choose not to enjoy the benefit of that. They may do this because they don't want to spoil their children, but that is an extreme position. The problem with taking that view is while they may choose not to live an extravagant life, at some point, they are going to pass on from this world. Assuming they leave their wealth to their children (and that is an assumption—not all parents do), the children will find out that they have inherited great wealth, and then, their children will actually have a problem with this because they won't be familiar with the lifestyle that can come with great wealth. It will be like they have won the lottery.

People who win the lottery invariably lose it. "About 70 percent of people who suddenly receive a windfall of cash will lose it within a few years, according to the National Endowment for Financial Education."[18] The majority of people who have a large and sudden financial windfall, through something like a lottery, end up losing it. Why? Because it is a shock to their lifestyle. Suddenly, they go from one financial position to another. That shock is unhealthy because they haven't learned how to adapt to it because it hasn't happened gradually. Suddenly, they're overwhelmed because they have the money, but they don't have the knowledge of how to be wealthy, and how to keep that money, and how to make that money grow. If somebody with wealth chooses to hide it from their children, eventually, the strategy will become unstuck, because the children will eventually find out. That's one extreme to be avoided.

The other extreme is those who live an extravagant life, where their children get whatever they want, like the couple arguing over a Bentley for their child. They set a very high bar, financially, for their lifestyle, which can be expensive to maintain and to sustain. There are a few reasons to avoid this. Let's consider very briefly the possibility that they might lose it. Many people follow the financial equivalent of "Better to have loved and lost to have never have loved before." People rarely say, "I'm not going to enjoy the full extent of my wealth because one day, I might not have it, and I don't want to get used to it." However, it's very difficult to take a backward step, financially, after having adjusted to a particular lifestyle.

Another problem with living a fantasy-type lifestyle, driven by wealth, is that it's very hard to bring up children with any values. If all children see is spending, spending, spending, and extravagance,

---

18 "Here's How Winning the Lottery Makes You Miserable." *Time.* Time. Web.

then they grow up believing that money is worthless, and they look elsewhere for meaning in their life. The trouble is, they don't always look for meaning in good places. If they're bored and they have no need to work, then they might end up looking for thrills that give them meaning, and some of those thrills can be very bad for them. They could end up taking unnecessary risks. They could end up depressed because their life has no meaning. Everybody needs meaning in their lives. The search for meaning is more difficult when you are at that extreme. You get up in the morning and you're always looking for the next thrill.

Additionally, if the activities in your life that bring you gratification are things that you spend money on, then you start to hit a sustainability problem because the more money you have (or spend), the *marginal* value of each dollar is lower. Spending becomes like a drug. When your thrills come from spending money, you keep needing to spend more money to get bigger thrills. You keep needing to go on a better and more expensive vacation than last time, get a better car, a better house. It's very much like a drug addiction. It never ends because you'll always be searching to have more and more. You'll never be gratified because the source of your gratification is money.

To avoid that, you need to find sources of gratification that are not financial, and that is the search for meaning. If you have a meaningful life, and if you get your thrills from doing something meaningful (as opposed to consumption and spending money), then those things are what can keep you going, and keep you feeling fulfilled in a sustainable manner.

Charles was born with a silver spoon in his mouth. He received the best of everything—lavish family vacations, the best education, and an expensive car (wrapped in a bow) for his sixteenth birthday. With a start like this, he would surely go far, his parents would say. After his father died suddenly at the young age of fifty-five, his mother took over control of the substantial family assets, established a board, and was able to grow the assets effectively. Unlike his elder sister, Charles was never really interested in the family business and completed a couple of university degrees while enjoying an expensive lifestyle.

According to the terms of the family trust, he received his share of the family wealth on his twenty-fifth birthday, and he began to *truly* live his dreams. For him, this meant going to the next level in terms of the trappings of ultra-high wealth: a private jet, mixing with A-listers. His mother was concerned, but this was tempered because fortunately, drugs were not one of Charles's vices. Spending, however, was. Charles also decided he had all the qualifications to be a venture capitalist, and invested in a large number of startups at seed and Series-A stage. Within two years, his wealth had either dwindled away due to spending or was illiquid—being tied up in speculative investments that would not deliver a return, if any, for several years.

It ended badly: his expensive toys had to be sold, and the family came to his assistance on a strictly limited and controlled basis. After six years in this "hellhole" of frugality, one of his tech investments resulted in a successful exit, but by then his net wealth was only a small fraction of what it had been, and he had learned a sobering lesson about life and the importance of diversification in investment.

It's very important to bring up children to be aware of wealth, but also to have a sense of what the purpose of that wealth is. They need to be brought up to be financially literate because the family has wealth, and at some point, they will be responsible for it. Right now, you are responsible for it, and previously, your parents were responsible for it. Eventually, you will transition it to the next generation. Give them the financial literacy to be aware of it, and to learn how to manage it on some scale, so that they are ready to manage the family assets in the future.

Finally, teach children humility regarding their family's wealth. They need to be aware that if they didn't make it, they have nothing to gloat about. Somebody else made it. They just happened to be born into their family. They could equally well have been born into a family that wasn't wealthy.

Raising Children with Wealth Action Step

Go to your *Transition Workbook* and follow along with the Raising Children with Wealth exercises. Take some time to consider what values you want your children to have regarding money, and identify how you will prepare them to live with wealth. Identify the rules established in your business. To download your complimentary workbook, go to www.DavidWerdiger.com/transition-workbook

CHAPTER 11

Cross-Generational Thinking

"When I was a boy of 14, my father was so ignorant I could hardly stand to have the old man around. But when I got to be 21, I was astonished at how much the old man had learned in seven years."

– Mark Twain

Cross-Generational Thinking

Cross-generational thinking requires that each generation develops an understanding of the other generations. Understand the differences in how each generation thinks. Learn to think like other generations. One does not need to agree with the thoughts and opinions of each generation; however, one must value the uniqueness of each generation and understand that their thoughts are worth considering.

Cross-generational thinking is about not letting generational labels define us. Rather, it's about engaging with other generations, learning from them, and understanding that they come from a different place. It is about trying to get the best of each generation.

Every generation will have positives and negatives in their approaches. Working within multiple generations, it's up to each generation to be honest with themselves and to seek to learn from the other generations.

The most important element of cross-generational thinking is that it works in all directions. This is *not* about the older generation acknowledging that the world is changing and that they must adapt and do things differently. It also requires the younger generation to acknowledge that they are not always right and that their way of doing things isn't always the best way. It is a feature of the younger/progressive generation that it thinks their way is the only way—that they are right and everybody else is wrong. They seek change for the sake of change. Cross-generational thinking has to go both ways. There needs to be a respect for differences, and in some cases, respect for age or maturity.

The Crashing Wall between Earning and Giving

In previous generations, there was an invisible wall between making and spending money, almost as if people had two distinct identities. They had their role when they were earning money, and they had their role when they were giving money away that was completely different. A business might act unethically or push the boundaries of good business practices, but nevertheless, when it came to philanthropy, they would be very generous. Because there was a disconnect between the two activities of making money and giving it away, people may not see that this behavior is rather incongruous. It was the norm to want to financially support a cause but not care about the way that money was made.

But when viewed together, there is a clear dissonance here. If you treat them as two completely different activities, then you are able to maintain a barrier. However, in contemporary generations, this wall is crashing down because the younger generations are not comfortable with the notion of acting one way when making money and a different way when giving it away.

It goes beyond that and extends even to the workplace. People have to get jobs to pay their bills, but the current generation wants more than just a pay packet: they want to work for a company that is also making the world a better place. This doesn't necessarily mean that they want to work for a nonprofit, rather they want to work for a company that is *consistent with their personal values.*

The human resource industry is shifting to adapt to this change. Millennials want to work for companies that meet their values. They are not just working to pay the rent or the mortgage or to meet their financial needs. Rather, they are working because they want to be in a workplace that is consistent with their own personal values. In this and other ways, we are seeing this wall between earning money and giving money away crashing down.

CSR, Ethical Investing, and Shared Value

The thinking since the 1970s is that corporations exist to *maximize shareholder value.* That is fancy-speak for increasing their share price. However, that is changing in a few ways. Many corporations have a division called "corporate social responsibly" (CSR) which reflects the sense that they are there for more than just making money. As "corporate citizens," they have a responsibility to also contribute to the betterment of society.

This is in part responding to the generational shift of employees wanting to go to a workplace and come home at the end of the day feeling satisfied that the world is just a little bit better as a result of the work they did. Even if it is work for a for-profit company, they still need that feeling.

The CSR industry itself is evolving. In its early days, a corporation might choose to donate a certain percentage of their profits to a benevolent cause. But this can end up being similar to the dissonance we discussed earlier, where someone is unethical in earning money, but donates from these same earnings. If Philip Morris decided to donate 10% of profits to lung cancer research, would we suddenly consider them a socially responsible corporate citizen?

Companies are taking this on in a more meaningful way, and this is driven from two different directions: firstly, employees wanting to be part of that and wanting to participate, for example where companies allow employees to spend a certain amount of their work hours on volunteering or pro-bono activities. The other is where companies themselves are seeking a more integrated approach to their CSR programs. For example, a bank is in the business of lending money out and keeping deposits, but also might create a banking product that is social.

In Australia, the ANZ Bank partners with the Salvation Army to deliver a savings program for low-income families that teaches children good saving habits and rewards them. Here, a bank is doing the opposite of what they usually do: banks make their money from lending and issuing credit, yet this bank is teaching people how to save. This is a banking approach to deciding to not just give away some of the profits that they have made. Rather, they are integrating their social responsibility into their core functions.

Ethical investing is an extension of this principle, driven by people who want to invest in companies that are doing good things for the world. Not only do younger generations care about business practices, they also care from a moral point of view about where they are investing money. People may not want to invest in the arms industry, the tobacco industry, or even the corn sugar industry. They may not invest in Coca-Cola shares because they feel their products contribute to the significant obesity problem that the US now faces.

It goes beyond not investing in companies that are doing harm. People want to actively fund companies that are specifically doing good and making improvements to the world. People don't necessarily have to give up returns in order to do this, which is good news, especially when we start talking about intergenerational issues. When different generations sit on the family investment committee, their philosophical approaches to investing can lead to conflict.

Corporations are evolving their goals from "maximizing shareholder value" to "being good corporate citizens," to "creating shared value"—pursuing financial success that also benefits society. In this latest iteration known as "collective impact," companies form complex alliances with others to create ecosystems that lead social change in the service of shareholder value.[19]

Social Enterprise

Another phenomenon in this space is known as "social enterprise." The traditional for-profit world and the nonprofit world represent two extremes. Social enterprise is occupying that gray space in between. A social enterprise is a company whose purpose is "to

---

19 @harvardbiz. "The Ecosystem of Shared Value." *Harvard Business Review.* 06 Sept. 2016. Web.

solve the most pressing societal problems."[20] These could also be considered for-profit companies that do not just have a corporate social responsibly program, but rather their entire purpose embodies a particular social responsibility and a cause. Importantly, they seek sustainability rather than being dependent on fundraising like many nonprofits.

These sorts of social enterprises have captured the attention of younger generations. Younger generations want to create, or work for, these types of companies. It allows them to really combine the earning side and the giving side. They can find a social enterprise that aligns with their interest and allows them to have the best of both worlds; they can earn a living, but at the same time, know that they are working for an organization that is there to make the world better. These are just a few key examples of how this wall between earning and giving has crashed down.

If you are in a multi-generational family, you may be thinking about what you should be doing, whether it's what you do with your life or how you choose to make philanthropic decisions on behalf of the family. Here is where there can be conflict because the older generation might have a different approach to this, but the younger generations wants to do things in a new way. This is where cross-generational thinking is essential.

The good news is that when doing ethical investing or investing in social enterprise, these initiatives are commercial. They don't require the investor to give up much, or anything, in terms of the returns they are seeking to meet both an investment criteria and a social criteria. Nevertheless, it does require a shift in mindset of the older generation to accept them, simply because they are a

20 "Social Enterprise Definition | Social Traders." *Social Traders.* Web.

departure from what has been done for decades ("the way we do things"). This can lead to significant shifts in investment policy. The older generation may decide that they are going to divest certain investments because they are no longer acceptable to the younger generation. They may decide to shift money into more ethical investments because they are considering the beliefs and values of the other generations.

Generation C

As mentioned in the first chapter, amongst all these generational labels, a new one has emerged: Generation C. As early as 2004, researchers noted them as a "cross-generational cohort," and the thinking about this generation has developed over the last few years. What does the "C" stand for? Anything you like: connected, community, collaboration, content. According to Google Think, "Gen C is a powerful new force in consumer culture…people who care deeply about creation, curation, connection, and community."[21] They are the digitally-savvy people—aged from children to the elderly—who are highly connected to the digital world and immersed in social media. This new kind of "generational" label goes beyond the traditional way of thinking about generations and focuses more on the group's values, which can bring people together from many generations.

Generation C is not a generation in the traditional sense, and certainly not in the sense we've been discussing. Rather, it's a *marketing construct.* It's a way to group and understand a set of consumers so that marketers can reach them and get them to

---

[21] "Meet Gen C: The YouTube Generation." *Think with Google.* Web.

buy their stuff. It doesn't seek to undo or reshape the way we view generations.

However, it is important for us because the fact that people of all ages can and have been able to connect with the digital world is important. For many, the digital world is a digital divide between generations. Many Baby Boomers don't know what to make of "the Facebook" and see it as yet another reason they *can't* connect with their children and grandchildren. However, Generation C shows us the way the digital world can actually be a cross-generational bridge. The younger generations were brought up with it—the challenge is there for the older generations to embrace it and use it as a way to connect.

Cross-Generational Thinking Action Step

Go to your *Transition Workbook* and follow along with the Cross-Generational Thinking exercises. Take some time to identify cross-generational attitudes regarding earning and giving money. To download your complimentary workbook, go to www.DavidWerdiger.com/transition-workbook

CHAPTER 12

The Search for Balance

"Extremes are easy. Strive for balance."
– Colin Wright

Early on in life, I was exposed to my parents' involvement in nonprofits. They were very community minded and very involved in supporting local community organizations, both financially and through being on committees and volunteering. Those were values that I saw from them growing up, and by osmosis, they became my values.

Having been involved in both the for-profit and nonprofit sectors, I was struck by a key difference between them. In the for-profit industry, the key things by which a company measures itself are revenues and profits. Those are the headline numbers by which they know if they are doing well.

However, in the nonprofit, rather than measuring size by revenues, they are measured by expenses. For a nonprofit, their expenses represent how much they spend achieving a certain social outcome. Of course, to be sustainable, a nonprofit has to raise money to cover their expenses, but the order of priorities is reversed.

Nonprofits don't raise ten million dollars and then decide how to spend it. Rather, they assess and quantify a social need and figure out how they are going to raise that money to meet that need.

These represent two opposite approaches to the very existence of an organization. When a for-profit measures itself by its revenues and profit, these are measures of the flow of funds from everything else around it. Effectively, a for-profit corporation measures itself by what it *takes;* revenues are the inward flow of money from anybody it sells to. Net profit is what is left net after deducting the cost of goods and expenses. *For-profit corporations measure themselves by what they take.*

Nonprofits, on the other hand, measure themselves by their expenses, which are the funds that they expend on others in pursuit of their goals. In effect, *they measure themselves by what they give.*

These two extremes can also be found in how people live their lives and how they measure their success. Do they measure themselves by what they take from those around them, or by what they give?

Hedonism and altruism are two polar opposite approaches to life. The hedonist is about personal gratification, and therefore, a hedonist is about what they take, how they enjoy life, and how they indulge in whatever life has to offer them. The opposite of the hedonist is the altruist. The altruist is there purely for others, which means the altruist is about what they give.

Nonprofit	For Profit
Expenses	Revenues & Profit
Giving	Taking
Meaning	Happiness
Altruism	Hedonism

These are extremes, and there is plenty of gray in between. The way to find balance is to recognize the extremes and then find your place in the middle.

Key to this is understanding the difference between happiness and meaning, so let's revisit an earlier diagram. Consider how wealth correlates with happiness. As wealth increases, once it reaches a certain threshold, happiness is unable to grow at the same rate as wealth. In American culture, with thanks to the great marketing industry, happiness has been closely linked to consumerism. It is about how much stuff you have and how much you buy. There is this notion in society that the more stuff you have, the happier you are. The fact is that many people define their happiness by consumption. Bigger is better. More is better.

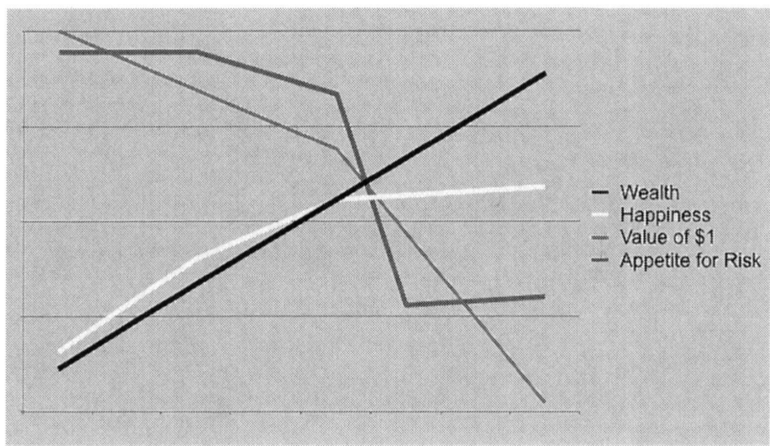

On the flip side of happiness is something that we call meaning. The best example of that is Victor Frankl, who wrote the book *Man's Search for Meaning.* He survived the Holocaust, survived a concentration camp, and the way he was able to survive was to recognize that despite what was taken from him during his experiences in a concentration camp, the one thing they couldn't take was his drive to have a meaningful life. "The one thing you can't take away from me is the way I choose to respond to what you do to me. The last of one's freedoms is to choose one's attitude in any given circumstance." The positive feeling that he had a purpose that would endure beyond his experience in the war is what kept him going. Most importantly, that feeling was something that nobody could take away from him, no matter what hardship he endured.

People find meaning through *giving*, so you can have a life that's a very difficult life or you can have a life that's not a very material life, but it can be a very meaningful life if you've been able to help others.

As the extremes, there is a contrast between for-profit and nonprofit, hedonism and altruism, happiness and meaning. It's not good to be at the extremes, whatever the case is, but it's important to recognize that there are limits to how much happiness you can get through consumption. We're not all fantastic altruists who will dedicate our lives to everybody else and not care about our own lives, so what we need to do is find that balance between giving and taking, between happiness and meaning.

Attitudes around this issue have changed between generations. As mentioned in the previous chapter, older generations used to have a very different approach to these two things. People would find balance by making sure that they had a reasonable dose of profit, and also a reasonable dose of nonprofit. People wanted to make money to be financially secure and have a good life, and also give away some of that money. More current thinking is that the two can be *combined.*

The other aspect to balance is active versus passive, which is particularly relevant when one has wealth. To what extent are you actively involved in the generation of profit and the distribution of nonprofit? My view is that it is also an area that needs balance. People end up being slaves to their own businesses and are so absorbed in them that they don't have time to smell the roses. On the flip side, there are people whose assets are entirely passive and all they do is get a dividend or a distribution on a regular basis and have very little involvement in growing their wealth or even maintaining their wealth. It's not good to be on either extreme because on one extreme, your business entirely absorbs you and you don't have a life. On the other extreme, you can potentially have a very big void in your life and nothing productive to do.

This dynamic can even apply to the giving or philanthropic side of you. One of the most powerful ways to connect generations is philanthropy. Sitting and writing checks to organizations is a very nice thing to do, but it can be a very cold form of giving. It's also good to sometimes immerse yourself more deeply and take a more active role in philanthropy. That might be through volunteering or it might be through sitting on a committee or on a board and contributing to the nonprofit in that way.

Occasionally you'll indulge and do something that's on one extreme, and then something on another extreme. Nobody lives their life entirely in the middle, but it's important to remember where you are and to know if you're going to do something that's extremely indulgent, fine you'll do it, but you'll know it's not your entire life. It may be something that you indulge in from time to time, but you won't make it your entire life because you will recognize that in doing so, you are going to one extreme rather than the other.

To find balance could be to either find that middle space where you've got a bit of everything or to bounce around between the extremes. The better way to find balance is to spend more time in the middle and less time in the extremes.

In a family business, it can be easy to lose balance and fall to one extreme or the other. During a transition, make sure that every generation's philosophies regarding earning and giving are recognized. Work together to find the middle ground that will bring happiness and meaning to your lives.

The Search for Balance Action Step

Go to your *Transition Workbook* and follow along with The Search for Balance exercises. Take some time to explore where you fall on the scale between earning and giving. To download your complimentary workbook, go to www.DavidWerdiger.com/transition-workbook

Conclusion

Transitions are never easy, and each one comes with its own set of challenges. Multi-generational family businesses face the unique challenge of transitioning roles and wealth from one generation to the next. With planning and awareness, you can experience a smooth and successful transfer that will allow the business to continue to thrive while also bringing happiness and meaning to all involved.

As you learned from this book, each generation must work respectfully with the other generations and value the different insights and communication styles each generation brings to the table. Each individual must have clear roles and expectations that fit their personal strengths and level of involvement. Additionally, the business must have clear values and goals regarding wealth and philanthropy.

While reading this book, I hope you also took the time to complete the exercises in the *Transition Workbook* to better identify your attitude toward other generations, wealth, values, opportunities, risk and balance. If you have not yet taken the time to enhance your understanding of you own perceptions about the family business, take the time now to visit www.DavidWerdiger.com/transition-workbook to access your copy of the *Transition Workbook.*

Now that you have completed the book and workbook, you have many of the tools necessary to achieve a smooth transition. However, multi-generational businesses are incredibly unique and complex. For a deeper understanding of how a multi-generational business thrives before, during, and after a transition, visit www.DavidWerdiger.com for additional resources.

Acknowledgements

Writing a book is a huge personal undertaking, but just like it takes a village to raise a child, it takes a team to put it all together and go from a spark of an idea to a published book. In completing this, my first book, I am filled with gratitude toward so many who have helped me through this journey in their own ways.

To my wife Adira, who saw potential in me that I didn't know existed and pushed me to help me realize it, who opened my eyes to the world of possibilities and new mountains that we can climb, and who made (and makes) me a better version of me.

To my dear parents, Nathan (may his memory be blessed) and Nechama (may she live a long and healthy life), who in their own way imbued me with the self-belief and ambition to achieve and who supported me every step of the winding road of my life journey.

To the coaches, mentors, advisors, and editors who rounded out my "team" through this journey to becoming an author: Lynn Garbers, Rory Carruthers, Carly Carruthers, Nimesh Madushanka, and others who gave me encouragement along the way.

To my friends and colleagues at Australian Jewish Funders, Jewish Funders Network, Private Wealth Network, 21/64, and ELI Talks who helped me form and develop many of the concepts that are the foundation of this book.

Finally, and specifically, to my late father. In the final year of his life, and particularly after his passing, it became clear to me quite how much an influence he was and how many decisions I made and directions I took in life were because of him. While he rarely said it to my face, he took every opportunity to tell others how proud he was of my achievements. He imbued me with deeply held values and convictions, which I embodied in my own way.

At his funeral, I said: "*Being the child of such a great achiever is simultaneously an honor and a heavy load to bear. How can we possibly hope to emulate him? It's a question I've asked myself many times, and I don't know the answer.*" Now I know the answer: to embody and continue their values, in our own way.

About the Author

David Werdiger is a #1 International Bestselling author, and the Founder and Chairman of Billing Bureau, one of the leading Australian Telecommunications Recurring Billing Software companies. He has been featured on ABC, NBC, CBS, FOX, The Wall St. Journal, USA Today and most recently he presented an ELI Talk titled "How to 'Have' Jewish Grandchildren." As an in-demand speaker, David travels the world sharing his ideas about business strategies, philosophies on life, Jewish culture, and philanthropy.

David has completed a Masters of Entrepreneurship and used his knowledge to expand several successful businesses in the Information Technology and Telecommunications industries. He currently mentors and advises family businesses, CEOs, and top-level entrepreneurs on how to successfully systemize their businesses so that they can increase revenue, scale, and even exit their business. David lives in Melbourne, Australia with his wife and five children.

Printed in Australia
AUOC02n0848120517
285653AU00001B/1/P

9 780986 103674